How to Be an Influence without Being Influenced

Student Journal

Andy Stanley and Stuart Hall

HOWARD
PUBLISHING CO.

Our purpose at Howard Publishing is to:
- *Increase faith* in the hearts of growing Christians
- *Inspire holiness* in the lives of believers
- *Instill hope* in the hearts of struggling people everywhere
Because He's coming again!

Max Q Student Journal © 2004 by Andy Stanley and Stuart Hall
All rights reserved. Printed in the United States of America

Published by Howard Publishing Co., Inc.
3117 North 7th Street, West Monroe, Louisiana 71291-2227
www.howardpublishing.com

04 05 06 07 08 09 10 11 12 13   10 9 8 7 6 5 4 3 2

Edited by Michele Buckingham
Interior design by Stephanie Denney Walker
Cover Design by LinDee Loveland and Stephanie Denney Walker

Library of Congress Cataloging-in-Publication Data

Stanley, Andy.
    Max Q : how to be influential without being influenced : student journal / Andy Stanley
and Stuart Hall.
        p. cm.
    Includes bibliographical references (p.).
    ISBN: 1-58229-361-9
    1. Christian teenagers—Religious life. 2. Influence (Psychology)—Religious
aspects—Christiantiy. I. Hall, Stuart, 1968- II. Title.

BV4531.3.S73 2004
248.8'3—dc22

                                                                        2004040618

Scripture quotations not otherwise marked are taken from the HOLY BIBLE, NEW INTERNA-
TIONAL VERSION®. Copyright © 1973, 1978, 1984 by the International Bible Society. Used by
permission of Zondervan Publishing House. All rights reserved. Scripture quotations marked
NASB are taken from the New American Standard Bible®, Copyright © 1960, 1962, 1963, 1971,
1972, 1973, 1975, 1977, 1995 by The Lockman Foundation. Used by permission. All rights
reserved. Scripture quotations marked *The Message Remix* are taken from THE MESSAGE. Copyright
© 1993, 1994, 1995, 1996, 2000, 2001, 2002. Used by permission of NavPress Publishing Group.

Contents

CONTENTS

Christ is the strongest, grandest, most attractive personality
ever to grace the earth. But a careless messenger
with the wrong approach can reduce all this magnificence
to the level of boredom.

JIM RAYBURN

Introduction

You are the greatest influence in another teenager's life. That's right. You. In fact, why don't you put this book down right now, go find a mirror, look at yourself, and say, "I am the greatest influence in another teenager's life."

Are you back? Did you do it?

Weirdo.

Here's the deal: Teenagers influence other teenagers. Big time. In fact, they often have more influence in each other's lives than parents or teachers or even youth pastors do.

You play a giant-sized role in the lives of your friends, your classmates, and the students you pass in the hall each day, whether you realize it or not. Whether your influence is positive or not. Whether your friends are believers— and especially if they're not.

It's not an easy role. And it's not risk free. Why? Because you live in a state of "Max Q." It's an unspoken part of your cultural and spiritual DNA. You can't see Max Q, but you can feel it. It's all around you.

What exactly is Max Q? The name of a new superhero? The title of the next Disney movie? A maximum-strength cotton swab?

Actually, Max Q is a term used in the space-shuttle program at Kennedy Space Center in Cape Canaveral, Florida. You see, roughly one minute after launch, a space shuttle must withstand a condition of extreme force known as *maximum dynamic pressure*—Max Q for short. This is the most critical point in flight from an aerodynamics perspective. It's when the most stress is placed on the vehicle. It happens just after the shuttle goes supersonic, at an altitude of 25,000 to 35,000 feet (five to seven miles up).

Dave King, former director of shuttle processing at KSC, sent us the following perspective from an astronaut friend of his: "I remember seeing equivalent airspeeds of around 455 knots. It's very noticeable to the crew because of something they don't model in the simulator: the wind noise. It's a whistling sound of the wind by the windows, I guess. It gets higher in volume and pitch as we approach Max Q, then the reverse happens as we get beyond it."

According to King, Max Q is the point where "you hope you did all your homework on the vehicle structure." Mission success demands that all systems on the space shuttle perform at the highest level in those moments. When designed properly, prepared carefully, and executed perfectly, the shuttle and its crew safely reach orbital velocity of 17,600 miles per hour at about eight-and-a-half minutes after launch.

We can think of no better illustration to describe what you and your friends experience in your day-to-day lives. You're in a constant state of maximum dynamic pressure. Your world moves at a pace of incredible proportion. Movies, music, and media constantly press you to embrace the world's perspective on beauty, sex, authority, behavior, money, success, and so much more. And that "whistling sound of the wind" grows in volume each day.

Go! No! Go! No!

Perhaps the most intense point of pressure lies in the arena of friendships. For most teenagers, fitting in, being accepted, and having a sense of belonging with a person or a group of people are top priorities. (We'll be honest with you. It's a priority for adults too.) You've probably seen other teenagers go to great lengths to gain the elusive and fleeting acceptance of their peers. Maybe you've gone to similar lengths. The desire for acceptance is a powerful motivation.

Often parents and youth leaders try to alleviate some of this pressure by encouraging you to choose friends from church, youth group, or other relatively small, controlled Christian circles. They barrage you with an onslaught of advice and wisdom concerning the perils of poor relationship choices:

"Choose your friends wisely."

"You are who you hang around with."

"Birds of a feather flock together."

"If you sleep with dogs, you're going to get fleas."

"If at first you don't succeed, skydiving is not for you."

(OK, maybe not that last one.)

Sound familiar? Don't get us wrong. Christian friends are great. You need them. They're absolutely critical to your spiritual growth and success. But the result of such advice is that subtly, over time, you end up distancing yourself more and more from your culture and from your peers who don't know Jesus. You separate yourself from the very teenagers who most desperately need what you have to offer: a relationship with Christ.

The Bible is clear: God wants us to love those people who don't know him personally. Jesus himself calls us to "go and make disciples" (Matthew 28:19). That's what he did when he walked this earth—and he didn't do it by keeping unbelievers at arm's length.

Do you see the contradiction? No wonder you feel so much pressure! The same adults who plead with you to only make friends with Christians also challenge you to be like Jesus and reach out to your unbelieving peers. You end up trapped in a fluctuating ping-pong game of Go! No! Go! No!

How do you respond? The potential exists for you to err on one of two extremes. On the one hand, you can determine to develop the healthiest of Christian friendships yet never seek to influence your unbelieving friends for the sake of Christ. The danger is that you may end up settling for being a "good" student—someone who doesn't drink, smoke, or chew, or date those who do—but never develops into the student of influence and greatness that God intends for you to be.

On the other hand, you can immerse yourself in your culture and develop friendships with lost peers without being anchored firmly in solid Christian relationships. The danger in this case is that you may cave in under the pressure, fall into sin, and suffer the negative consequences that come from making bad choices. God doesn't want you to risk your character, your integrity, and your spiritual well-being for the sake of his kingdom. He has not called you to be reckless.

He has, however, called you to influence your friends. It's the right thing to do. And the fact is, most of the time the right thing to do is hard. The right thing to do is full of risk. There are no promises of ease or safety in following Jesus. No guarantees. Just his promise that he "will never leave you or forsake you." That he is with you always.

Using This Journal

We have written the *Max Q Student Journal* (and its companion book for youth ministers, *Max Q: Developing Students of Influence*) to help you do the right—albeit difficult—thing. We're convinced that God's intention is for you to become a student who is spiritually influential. A student who is both willing *and* spiritually strong enough to step across lines that some consider taboo in order to influence other teens for Christ. A student who is not swayed by culture, popular opinion, or temptation but rather shines as a light in dark places. A student who maintains strong accountability with Christian friends while developing significant relationships with lost teenagers who desperately need Jesus.

Easier said than done, right?

That's why we've written this journal. It's designed to help you discover what it means to become spiritually influential and to provide you with the tools you need to begin that process.

One of our main goals is to shift your thinking from traditional concepts of evangelism (knocking on doors, inviting people to big events) to what we believe is a more biblical concept: *disciplism* ("disciple" with an "ism"). That's a word we've coined to connect the two parts of Jesus' command: "Go" and "make disciples." Disciplism involves more than making a one-time connection with unbelievers. It means investing your life into the lives of your lost peers for the sake of influencing them for the gospel.

Lost teenagers don't need more evangelism programs or outreach efforts. They need relationships with strong Christian students, students of real character and substance, who will do more than invite them to a church event and hope for the best. Our years of experience in youth ministry have made one thing crystal clear: Lost teenagers rarely give God a chance unless a Christian peer has developed real relational leverage with them. Teenagers who come to Christ do so because a Christian friend has loved them enough to lead them to Jesus one step at a time.

In the pages to come, we will explore what a real student of influence looks like. We will attempt to unravel and understand influence as a principle. We will examine the life of Christ to see how he modeled relational influence.

We will spend most of our time, however, diving into six key principles that we believe are critical for you to become spiritually influential:

- developing godly convictions and standards
- establishing your relationship with God as your top priority
- maintaining accountability with other Christians
- loving your lost peers radically and unconditionally

- sustaining your influence with your unbelieving friends
- leveraging your influence for the sake of the gospel

We've divided the journal into ten weeks, with each week containing five days of material for you to consider. The idea is for you to go through one section of the journal each day (Monday through Friday) for ten weeks. On the weekends we encourage you to apply your discoveries from the previous five days through an experiential learning task (EXP for short). EXP is specifically designed to solidify in your heart and mind what you've been learning about becoming a student of influence.

The Q Text

Each day begins with a passage of scripture that we call the *Q Text*. You will need to get out your Bible and carefully read the Q Text, making sure you understand the meaning of the verses. What do they have to do with you and influence? To maximize your comprehension, ask yourself these questions:

- *What do I need to know from this passage?* (It's a good idea to get in the habit of summarizing scripture in your own words.)

- *Why is this important?* (It doesn't really matter what you know unless what you know really matters!)

- *What should I do about it?* (Application, not information, leads to transformation.)

- *How can I remember this?* (There's a saying that goes "I saw, and I forgot. I heard, and I remembered. I did, and I understood." Experiencing the truth is invaluable if you want that truth to stick.)

The Q Test

The Q Test is comprised of two or three critical questions based on the thoughts presented in the Q Text. These questions are purposely crafted to create tension in your mind and heart. To ignore them is to bypass the process of influence! Instead, be sure to answer these questions as honestly and as intentionally as possible.

The Q Point

Each day the Q Test is followed by several paragraphs of information and insight designed to help you understand, personalize, and apply the principles of influence you are discovering. We call this section the *Q Point.* (We could have called it the *Q Tip,* but would you have taken it as seriously?) As you read and consider this section, make notes, record any questions you have, and be sure to journal your thoughts and feelings at the end.

Preparing for Launch

At the risk of sounding melodramatic, we want to warn you: Choosing to become a student of influence is not for the faint of heart. Becoming influential in the life of an unbelieving friend will tax every ounce of your energy. It will draw on every bit of wisdom you have. You will most likely fail at some point along the way. You will grow weary. You will doubt. Max Q will press in on every side.

But you can survive. You can even thrive! How? By deciding right now to commit yourself to achieving the same level of excellence that NASA engineers must apply each time they launch the space shuttle. By determining to surpass the typical standards of goodness in order to become a student of greatness. By developing balance, passion, courage, and the wisdom that comes through adversity. By recognizing that a "student of influence" is an attitude as well as an outcome.

This journal represents a launch pad into the life that God designed for you—a life of knowing him and making him known to a lost world. Whether you successfully complete your mission or not depends in large part on what you do after you turn this page.

Are you ready to start the countdown?

The Truth about Influence

The great reformer Martin Luther once said,

> If I profess with the loudest voice and clearest exposition every portion
> of the truth of God except precisely that point which the world and the
> devil are at that moment attacking, I am not confessing Christ. Where
> the battle rages, there the loyalty of the soldier is proved.
>
> And to be steady on all the battlefield is merely flight and disgrace if
> he flinches at that point.

As a Christian teenager, you can spend all your time participating in the greatest youth programs in town. You can devote all your energy to becoming the most well-behaved student within the four walls of the church. But that's not the battlefront. The point of attack comes elsewhere. The battle takes place at precisely that point where you touch the lives of your lost friends and influence those peers who desperately need Christ.

Have you flinched at this point? Many Christian students (and adults) do. May you flinch no more.

Granting Permission
Becoming a Student of Influence

Let people feel the weight
of who you are
and let them deal with it.

JOHN ELDREDGE

Granting Permission
Becoming a Student of Influence

It was Saturday morning, February 1, 2003. In perhaps the greatest tragedy in space-exploration history, seven courageous heroes lost their lives that day. The space shuttle Columbia, returning from a sixteen-day mission to outer space, reentered the earth's atmosphere at more than eighteen times the speed of sound and, only minutes from its scheduled landing, disintegrated some 207,000 feet over Texas.

Most of us will never forget where we were on that fateful morning. Our hearts broke and mourned with the families of those seven astronauts, many of whom were gathered on a runway at Kennedy Space Center in Florida awaiting their loved ones' safe return. Columbia and her crew were lost only sixteen minutes from home.

It will most likely take the sharpest and brightest minds years to determine the specific cause of this horrific loss. We may never know the full extent of the truth. But one thing is certain: Columbia, in the midst of experiencing maximum dynamic pressure, when she needed to be the strongest, was weak.

Perhaps her weakness was minute; perhaps it was greater than we'll ever know. Regardless of the degree, the fact remains that when the heat and pressure reached its highest intensity, Columbia's integrity was compromised.

The vehicle was unable to withstand Max Q. And what was to be a defining, triumphant moment became a terribly destructive one.

It's not much of a stretch to parallel the state of Max Q as it relates to space exploration to the pressures you face as a Christian teenager. In fact, the comparisons are hauntingly similar.

We don't have to tell you about the intense pressure that society exerts on you and your friends through music, television, movies, the media—and one another. You know it well. You experience it every day. And you probably understand (at least in theory) that in order for you to withstand that pressure without being influenced by it, you must live at a very high level of wisdom, purity, and courage.

Unfortunately, many Christian students are not trained to operate at that level. For years we have watched as Christian homes and youth ministries have sent graduates headlong into Max Q. Too often the results have been as tragic as the loss of the space shuttle. Reeling under the intense pressure, many students get suckered into making poor choices. Or they become magnetized to lifestyles that don't match their stated belief system. In fact, according to statistics, over three-fourths of Christian teenagers after graduating from high school will abandon the church—and possibly even their faith.[1]

Will you be a statistic—or a catalyst for change?

Will you be the one influenced by others—or the one who influences others for Christ?

Day
ONE

🗩 Text

Read 1 Corinthians 5:1–11.

🗩 Test

What is the problem Paul addresses in this letter to the Corinthian church? _____

_____

_____

_____

_____

How were the Corinthians handling this problem? According to Paul, was their approach right or wrong? _____

_____

_____

_____

_____

_____

PART ONE:
THE TRUTH ABOUT
INFLUENCE

🗩 Point

We're not rocket scientists, but we think the odds are pretty high that you have at least a few acquaintances who are not Christians. And you probably feel a certain tension regarding these friends. Is it OK to get close to them? Will you be judged by God or your Christian peers for reaching out to unbelievers? Should you feel guilty for having friends who are lost?

Here's the bottom line: Is it God's will for you to have non-Christian friends?

Apparently the early church battled with this very dilemma. Paul specifically addressed the hyperreaction of the church in Corinth to a challenge he had previously given. His response to their reaction is recorded in 1 Corinthians 5:

> I wrote you in my letter not to associate with immoral people; I did not at all mean with the immoral people of this world, or with the covetous and swindlers, or with idolaters, for then you would have to go out of the world. But actually, I wrote to you not to associate with any so-called brother if he is an immoral person, or covetous, or an idolater, or a reviler, or a drunkard, or a swindler—not even to eat with such a one.
> (1 Corinthians 5:9–11 NASB)

Even though his earlier letter is not included in the New Testament, Paul implies in verse 9 that he had previously written to the church in Corinth, instructing them not to associate with immoral people. Apparently the Corinthian church misinterpreted this

Should you feel guilty for having friends who are lost?

directive. For some reason the Corinthian believers—like so many of us—thought that Paul's message to separate themselves from immoral people meant they were to steer clear of people who did not know God. They assumed he meant they should put as much distance as possible between themselves and the "pagans."

Paul, however, was not referring to people who didn't know God. And in this passage in 1 Corinthians 5, he cleared up the misunderstanding—for the Corinthians and for us. When he said that believers should not associate with immoral people, *he did not mean the immoral people of this world*. He was referring

GRANTING PERMISSION

to people who claim to be Christians (so-called brothers) who continue in the active practice of sin. Paul says we should not even eat with such people!

Have you maintained a cool distance between yourself and your lost friends because you've assumed you shouldn't have relationships with "sinners"? What do you think about that approach now? Journal your thoughts here.

PART ONE:
THE TRUTH ABOUT
INFLUENCE

Day
TWO

Text

Read 1 Corinthians 5:9–11.

Test

How did the Corinthians misinterpret Paul's initial instruction? _____

_____

_____

_____

_____

What could they accomplish by only going "out of the world"? _____

_____

_____

_____

Point

It seems that Paul sensed the absurdity of the response of the Corinthian church when he said that in order to disassociate with immoral people, we would have to "go out of the world." In other words, lost people are all around you. You would have to leave this planet to get away from them. If you don't want to associate with lost teenagers, you need to move to Mars.

Now understand, we are writing this not only as youth ministers; we're also parents. Between the Stanley and Hall families, we have six children. We recognize and take seriously the pressures of the world our children live in. With our wives we pray constantly for their purity of heart and mind. We work extremely hard to protect them from the negative influences that can creep in so subtly through unhealthy friendships, television, movies, and music.

GRANTING PERMISSION

But we have to ask ourselves: What's our role as parents? Isn't it to ground our children in the things of God so they can stand on their own two feet one day and be influential without being influenced? Isn't the major task of their existence on this earth, like our own, to know God and make him known?

Let's make this very personal: Isn't that the major task of *your* existence?

What good are we as parents if we teach our children to run from the major task of their lives? What good are we as youth ministers and authors if we tell you to do the same?

Granted, the easiest thing is to get out of the world. To hide. To safely stay behind the four walls of the church. We won't kid you: Being *in* the world but not "of the world" (John 17:15–16) is tough. But who is going to reach your friends for Christ if you are running from them? Journal your thoughts.

PART ONE:
THE TRUTH ABOUT
INFLUENCE

Day THREE

🗨 Text

Read 1 Corinthians 5:11–13.

🗨 Test

Who were the Corinthians not to associate with? _____

_____

_____

_____

Why did Paul want the Corinthians to avoid these people? _____

_____

_____

_____

_____

🗨 Point

Paul introduces a concept in these verses that he would expound on in future letters: church discipline. The heart of it is quite simple. Christians must be accountable to God and to other Christians. They must judge those within the church—not those outside the church.

Let's make it personal. You and your Christian friends must hold one another accountable for living according to biblical standards. That's your responsibility as brothers and sisters in Christ. At the same time, you must not judge unbelieving friends who act and think immorally; God reserves that responsibility for himself.

Here is a major announcement brought to you by the God of the universe: Lost people are going to act lost—because they are lost! They have never

GRANTING PERMISSION

made the choice to play by God's rules, so they can't be expected to. You can't be their judge.

What you *can* do is love them and seek to be influential in their lives. Youth leaders and others may have nailed a No Trespassing sign on relationships with unbelievers, but that sign does not reflect the heart of God.

We're not implying that you should be reckless and put your life at risk by becoming a "companion of fools" (Proverbs 13:20). It is vital that you have strong and healthy relationships with Christian friends. In fact, those relationships should be a priority. But neither can you ignore God's challenge to reach out to your unbelieving friends. To do so would be as wrong and destructive as ignoring God's wisdom to not walk with fools.

That means you have a daunting, yet urgent, task: You must become a student who can be influential without being influenced. Admittedly, this is a high-wire act that must be walked with balance and precision. But you must embrace the tension and learn how to live with it without being destroyed by it.

Are you willing to take on this assignment? What do you see as the major hurdles to your becoming a student of influence? Write down what is in your heart.

PART ONE:
THE TRUTH ABOUT
INFLUENCE

_____

_____

_____

_____

_____

_____

_____

_____

_____

_____

Day
FOUR

🗨 Text

Read Proverbs 27:19.

🗨 Test

What does your heart reflect about you? What are your strongest passions and desires? _____

_____

_____

_____

_____

_____

_____

Would you say that one of the desires of your heart is to become influential in the lives of your lost friends? Why or why not? _____

_____

_____

_____

_____

🗨 Point

As a Christian student, you have the rare potential to order your life in a way that will not only affect the lives of other human beings; it may even change the course of history. The friends you influence today are the world changers and world influencers of tomorrow.

Before you can begin to influence the hearts of others, however, you must first examine what's in your own heart. When it's dark inside, that darkness will eventually manifest itself outside. When you neglect the deepest parts of yourself, that neglect will begin to affect those parts that are most visible.

The most influential students work from a place of passion and character within their own hearts. If they don't, they can't inspire, they can't lead, and they can't model the influential life.

> **The most influential students work from a place of passion and character.**

It takes courage to act and lead from the heart. To do so means that you are standing and living for things you believe in—things that burn like a branding iron in your soul. You are professing values that are important to you. But know this: You will always be a target when you live and lead that way. In fact, go ahead and draw a huge bull's-eye on yourself right now, because your desire to be a student of influence will draw friendly and unfriendly fire. There will be youth pastors and parents and other students who will not understand what you're doing, and some of them will be pretty good shots.

Living and leading from the heart definitely brings a degree of tension and pain. But to not lead from the heart has consequences that are even more painful. Not leading from the heart results in a divided life. Affirming something inwardly, yet behaving in a completely different way outwardly. Living in a constant state of awareness of what you should *be* versus what you are, what you *should* be doing versus what you *are* doing. How excruciating! Unfortunately, many Christian students feel this pain today. Maybe you feel it.

Mark it down: Choosing to become a student of influence will lead you into some scary places. You'll learn things about your heart that you haven't had to face before. Quite a few bogeymen lurk beneath the shallow ideas of modern friendship, evangelism, and ministry to teenagers. But to keep them below the surface is the equivalent of giving Sammy Sosa more creatine or cork—they will only grow stronger.

What's in your heart? Are there dark things there that keep you from living and leading in a way that will draw your friends to Christ? What are you going to do about it? Journal your thoughts.

Day
FIVE

Text

Read Jeremiah's prayer in Jeremiah 32:17–19.

Test

According to this passage, how did God make the heavens and the earth?

_____

_____

How did Jeremiah view the purposes and deeds of God? How do you think having such a view impacted the way he lived? _____

_____

_____

_____

_____

_____

_____

PART ONE:
THE TRUTH ABOUT
INFLUENCE

Point

Does it really matter whether or not you become a student of influence in your world? Is it really necessary to have such a lofty goal? Wouldn't it be OK to dream a little smaller?

Small dreams are great for certain things. For example, if you dream small, you will probably always meet your goal. You will probably have an easy time finding a measurement for your success. And you'll almost certainly have a lock on a life of comfort and least resistance.

Small dreams are great for other things too. They're great if you're not interested in changing or moving beyond the status quo. Small dreams are great if you're convinced that the only people who have spiritual influence are preachers, singers, and missionaries. Small dreams are great if you enjoy mediocrity. If you're highest ambition is to be a "good" teenager, then go ahead and dream a tiny dream.

There's one big problem with such a small dream: Our God isn't small. And if God isn't small, then his dreams aren't small. You are going to have to dream big if you want your heart to be in tune with God's heart.

If your vision for your life is to simply survive the culture and its pressures, ask yourself: Is that a God-sized dream? Is that really what God envisions for you and your life here on earth?

The truth is, God has a big dream for you. It's much bigger than keeping your life nice and safe and tidy and "religious."

Here's the bottom-line question: How big is your God? Your answer is critical. It has everything to do with whether or not you become a student of influence. Take time right now to write down what you are thinking and feeling about God's greatness and his plan for your life.

EXP In many ways this matter of becoming a student of influence represents a fork in the road for you. You can choose to dream big, lead from the heart, pour yourself into others, become a person of real character and substance, and build bridges of relationship to your unsaved friends. Or you can go the way of so many Christian students and depend on your youth pastor and the programs at your church to reach other teenagers. Which road will you take?

A movie that has been popular with our two families in recent years is *First Knight*, an account of King Arthur's Camelot from a unique perspective. In one great scene, a huge festival is being held in Camelot. One of the attractions of the festival is a gauntlet—an extreme obstacle course of sharp, swinging blades; huge logs and stones; and constantly moving platforms. Men put on the equivalent of a bed mattress and try to walk from one end of the gauntlet to the other without getting knocked off or—worst-case scenario—being decapitated.

The soon-to-be queen promises a kiss to any man who can conquer the gauntlet, a feat that no one has ever accomplished. That's when Lancelot (played by Richard Gere) steps up and, with no padding at all, defeats the gauntlet—thus becoming the first person to do so and winning the prize.

King Arthur (Sean Connery) is amazed at Lancelot's feat of courage, athleticism, and quick thinking, so he strikes up a conversation that would serve us all well to consider. When King Arthur asks Lancelot how he conquered the gauntlet, Lancelot answers, "It is not hard to know where the danger is if you watch it coming."

"Others have tried and failed. You were the first," King Arthur says.

"Perhaps fear made them go back when they should have gone forward," Lancelot responds.[2]

PART ONE:
THE TRUTH ABOUT
INFLUENCE

The state of Max Q exists in your teenage world as surely as it exists at the edge of the earth's atmosphere. It's dangerous, to be sure. But don't let fear grip your heart. Don't go back when you should go forward. To live the way God created you to live, to reach out to your lost friends the way God intends for you to reach out, you must face the danger. It isn't hard to know where the danger is when you can see it coming.

You can begin today to rise to a new level of expectation in your life. You can become an influencer among your peers and in your world.

Are you afraid? Then push forward!

Here's your EXP task for this weekend: Go to your local video store and rent the movie *First Knight*. As you watch it, look for the answer to these questions:

What happens when Lancelot discovers something to live for? _____

_____

_____

_____

_____

_____

_____

What motivates him to do the things he does in his life? _____

_____

_____

_____

_____

_____

_____

_____

GRANTING PERMISSION

Knowing What to Expect
Lessons from the Master Influencer

The purpose of the church cannot
be to survive or even to thrive but to serve.
And sometimes servants die in the serving.

ERWIN RAPHAEL MCMANUS

Knowing What to Expect
Lessons from the Master Influencer

Let's be honest: To the large majority of your unbelieving friends, the church has a reflection problem.

Lost students are not ticked off at a building. They're not apathetic toward your youth-group room. Most are not even angry with God. No, unbelieving teenagers distance themselves from *Christians.* They reject the picture of the church they see reflected in the lives of the believers they know.

If you don't believe the church at large has a reflection problem, sit down with your friends at church or youth group and ask this question: "Based on what you have seen and heard, how do you think our church would fill in this blank: The Christian life is _____?"

Their answers (and yours) will probably astonish you. Granted, perception is the cruelest form of reality. But the students we interviewed for this book responded across the spectrum, from one extreme—"The Christian life is a bunch of rules, a list of dos and don'ts"—to the opposite extreme—"It's whatever makes you feel good." And these were Christian students!

Can you imagine what your unbelieving peers think?

The Bible clearly teaches that the church is an extension—and should be a reflection—of the person of Jesus Christ. The problem is, too many Christian students (and adults) are failing to reflect the purpose and personality of Jesus to a lost world. More times than not, they're reflecting their own purposes and personalities—or perhaps the purposes and personalities of their respective churches. No wonder there's a reflection problem!

To become a student of influence, you must first become a person whose life accurately reflects the purpose and personality of Jesus. The key question, then, is this: When your friends look in the mirror of your life, what do they see?

Is it Jesus?

Day
ONE

Q Text

Read Acts 8:1–3 and Acts 9:1–6.

Q Test

Who or what was Saul trying to destroy by persecution? _____

_____

_____

_____

According to Jesus' question in verse 4, who was Saul persecuting? What do you think is significant about this answer?_____

_____

_____

_____

_____

_____

_____

_____

**PART ONE:
THE TRUTH ABOUT
INFLUENCE**

Q Point

In Acts 8 we see that Saul stood by and watched as Stephen, a believer, was violently stoned to death for his faith in Christ. But Saul was more than an innocent bystander. He was the one giving approval for the murder. He even helped by guarding the robes of the men who were doing the actual stone throwing (Acts 22:20).

Saul hated Christ, Christianity, and most of all, Christians. His sole purpose in life was to snuff out the movement of Christianity once and for all.

But look again at Acts 8:1–3. Although Saul was leading the persecution against the church, notice what that did *not* mean: He was not vandalizing facilities or painting graffiti on walls. He wasn't burning down buildings. He was dragging *people* to prison!

Now turn to Acts 9:1–5. When Saul was traveling to Damascus to arrest more Christians, he had an amazing encounter. A sudden light flashed, and Saul fell to the ground. Then he heard a voice—the voice of Jesus—asking, "Saul, Saul, why do you persecute me?"

Your task is to reflect the personality and purpose of Jesus to your world.

Persecute *me*? Saul wasn't persecuting Jesus. He was persecuting Jewish Christians. Jesus was already dead, alive again, and gone. Saul never even met him. How could he be persecuting Jesus?

Here's how: Jesus was so closely associated with the church that when Saul persecuted people (the church), he was persecuting Jesus himself.

The church, you see, is not a building. It's not an institution. It's an extension of Jesus. That means that the church should reflect the personality of Jesus. It should have his same purpose. And despite what our distorted reflections convey, that purpose is not fuzzy. Jesus came to earth for a single purpose: "to seek and to save what was lost" (Luke 19:10). To reconnect the disconnected. To bring glory to the Father in heaven by bridging the gap between sinful people and a holy God.

As a Christian student, you are the church to the teenagers around you. You're not the church of tomorrow; you're the church of *right now*. And your task is to reflect the personality and purpose of Jesus to your world right where you are.

KNOWING WHAT TO EXPECT

How are you doing? Spend some time thumbing through Matthew, Mark, Luke, and John and write down what you observe about the purpose and personality of Jesus. Journal your thoughts about how well you reflect these traits in your own life.

PART ONE:
THE TRUTH ABOUT
INFLUENCE

🗩 Text

Read John 2:1–11.

🗩 Test

Why do you think Jesus and his disciples attended the wedding? What does that say to you about Jesus?_____

_____

_____

_____

_____

Why did Jesus turn the water into wine? _____

_____

_____

_____

_____

🗩 Point

The Gospel accounts make clear that Jesus is not the meek, mild, maybe slightly boring individual so many people peg him for. Rather, his personality can be summed up best in these four characteristics:

1. Authentic

For Jesus, authenticity was paramount. He was all about the truth—which meant he was always battling against the Pharisees, the pretentious, pious, and unauthentic religious leaders of his day.

How does this relate to you? Unfortunately, many unbelieving teenagers think that Christian students are as pretentious, pious, and unauthentic as the

KNOWING WHAT TO EXPECT

Pharisees and Michael Jackson's nose. To accurately reflect Jesus, you must be authentic. You must show that you hurt, you fear, you care. That you don't have all the answers. That you're not hiding behind Sunday-school clichés. That you live in the real world with a real God who is real life.

2. Relevant

Being relevant means "using what is cultural to communicate what is timeless."[1] If Jesus was anything, he was always relevant to his culture. Whether relating a biblical concept to sowing, reaping, fishing, a widow's coin, or a lost sheep, Jesus used what people were familiar with to engage their hearts and minds and communicate truths that had both eternal implications and practical applications.

Your friends are looking for relevance. They want to know how truth relates to them in their world. They want to see the God-life lived out in the here and now and not just spoken of in the sweet by and by. Your challenge is to meet them where they are and learn how to use what is cultural to communicate what is timeless.

3. Enjoyable

One thing the Gospels make clear: Jesus was always the life of the party. People wanted to be near him. Even children and sinners felt welcome around him.

As a reflection of Jesus, you should be the kind of person your lost peers enjoy being around. If you're walking around your school with a serious face, a chip on your shoulder, and no joy in your step, then you most definitely have missed the heart of God. To be like Jesus, you must enjoy life—and be enjoyable!

4. Accepting

In at least nine places in the Gospels, Jesus is shown sharing a meal with a person or group of people other than his disciples. Interestingly, in seven of those nine times, Jesus is eating with people who were considered the worst sinners of their day. Tax collectors. Prostitutes. Only twice do we see him eating with religious people. What does that tell you about the personality of Christ?

If there is a characteristic that Jesus exemplified more than any other, it is acceptance. Jesus was always befriending people who had shady or difficult pasts. He was accepting of those people who were considered socially or relationally off-limits by others. He is the example to follow for loving and accepting every one of your lost peers.

Do you reflect acceptance, authenticity, and the other characteristics of Christ's personality? Journal your thoughts.

KNOWING WHAT TO EXPECT

Day
THREE

⬚ Text

Read John 15:18–21 and John 16:1–4.

⬚ Test

Who do you think Jesus is talking about when he says "the world"? Why will the world hate his disciples? _____

_____

_____

_____

_____

Based on these passages, do you think persecution is a good or bad thing? Why?_____

_____

_____

_____

_____

_____

PART ONE:
THE TRUTH ABOUT
INFLUENCE

⬚ Point

If you are going to become a student of influence, then you need to know what to expect. You can't rush headlong into maximum dynamic pressure under false expectations or with naïve assumptions. NASA astronauts would never do that; their lives are at stake. Spiritually speaking, so is yours.

Jesus understood this. That's why he told his disciples what was just around the corner for them as they began the process of disciplism. He didn't sugarcoat it. He said quite plainly that they would be hated, rejected, and worse. He wanted them to anticipate these reactions so that when they encountered them, they wouldn't be surprised, afraid, intimidated, or thrown off course.

The same principles that Jesus laid out for the disciples hold true for you. As you become a student of influence, you *will* face rejection and ridicule. As you invest your life into the lives of your unbelieving friends, you will encounter resistance, at the very least—and maybe much worse.

Understand, your lost friends have a perspective on life that is radically different from yours. They view faith, relationships, the opposite sex, choices, parents, authority figures, even themselves, through a frame of reference that promotes self as god. It's as if they're looking through the big end of a telescope to see the world: Everything reduces to self. When you start living the Christ-life before them, you threaten that perspective. You flip the telescope, causing them to see themselves in reality.

> **As you become a student of influence, you *will* face rejection and ridicule.**

But then, that's exactly what's supposed to happen. When Jesus ascended to heaven, he set in motion a plan to redeem mankind that depends upon believers living out authentic Christian lives before a lost and needy world. The bottom line is that God wants to use your life to convict your unbelieving peers. That's been his plan all along.

How will your friends react when they begin to sense that they are wrong or don't measure up? Most likely they won't admit it. Our natural human tendency is to deny or reject the standard by which we're being judged. Think about it. If you believe that you weigh 200 pounds and you get on a scale that says you weigh 225, what is your immediate reaction going to be? You will probably think that the scale is wrong (denial). Or you'll get angry at the scale

KNOWING WHAT TO EXPECT

and want to throw it away (rejection). Surely there is something wrong with the scale, not your weight!

Well, to your lost friends, *you* are that scale. When you become a student of influence, your very presence is a constant reminder to them of everything they are not. That's why they react the way they do.

What reactions have you been getting from your unbelieving peers? What do those reactions say about you? Journal your thoughts.

PART ONE:
THE TRUTH ABOUT
INFLUENCE

💬 Text

Read John 16:5–11 .

💬 Test

Who is the "he" referred to in these verses? _____

_____

_____

What are the three things the Holy Spirit will do? Why will he do these three things? _____

_____

_____

_____

_____

_____

_____

_____

💬 Point

As you become a student of influence, you can expect to be rejected by unbelieving friends. Here are three reasons why:

1. You are a foreigner.

Speaking to his disciples only hours before his betrayal and arrest, Jesus said, "If you belonged to the world, it would love you as its own. As it is, you do not belong to the world, but I have chosen you out of the world. That is why the world hates you" (John 15:19).

If you were like everyone else in your high school, then you would be accepted as such. But Jesus' point is clear: As a follower of Christ, you are not like everyone else. You are an alien. You're like E.T. walking through the school hall. You stick out like Marilyn Manson at a George Strait concert.

2. *Your unbelieving friends don't have a relationship with Christ.*

Jesus continued: "They will do such things because they have not known the Father or me" (John 16:3).

In rejection, the issue is a lack of relationship, not a lack of information. Unbelievers don't believe that Jesus is who he claimed to be. Or they believe, but they have never trusted in him or submitted their lives to him. The whole idea of submitting to Christ—of placing their lives under the authority of an invisible God—seems incomprehensible and threatening. Rejection, then, is the result of unbelieving students not knowing Jesus. You are guilty simply by association.

3. *The Holy Spirit is at work convicting your friends through you.*

We touched on this point yesterday. When you live out the Christ-life before your peers, the barrier that separates them from a holy God grows increasingly evident to them. You don't have to continually berate your friends about sinful habits or lifestyles. What will cause sin to become more noticeable will be the striking contrast between their compromised lives and your life of freedom in Christ.

Why do you think your friends practically beg you to sin? Why the constant, never ending cascade of Max Q: "Come on, just one drink . . . just one drag . . . just one sniff"? Because you represent everything they know they could and should be—and they hate the comparison. They want to blur the contrast.

**PART ONE:
THE TRUTH ABOUT
INFLUENCE**

Which teenagers will reject you the most vehemently? Not those "pagan" friends who have never stepped foot in church, whose lives are in complete shambles. No, the most intense rejection will come from those students who grew up in church and have since abandoned it. It will come from those teens who have experienced enough of religion to make them wary and skeptical. It will come from those who have seen the worst in people and mistakenly connect their bad experiences with God.

Be forewarned: Jesus was rejected. So were the disciples. You will be too.

How will you respond? Are you secure enough in Christ to be able to handle rejection? What does being rejected say about you? Take a moment to write down your thoughts.

Day FIVE

Text

Read John 14:27.

Test

What is the promise of this verse? _____

_____

_____

How does peace of this world differ from God's peace? _____

_____

_____

_____

_____

Point

All this talk of rejection could seem to be grounds for frustration and discouragement. You may wonder, *Is influence worth the cost?* Max Q is tough enough without a big heap of rejection thrown in for good measure!

The truth is, Jesus doesn't promise us a storm-free life; he promises us peace in the midst of every storm. And biblical faith is riveted in believing that God is who he says he is and that he will do what he has promised to do. His promises are like a bridge that will carry you from being a student of wishful thinking to a student of mountainlike faith.

The peace Jesus promises in John 14:27 is not based on the usual things like circumstances or how you feel. No, God's peace is similar to joy. It is an unswerving condition of the soul. You can walk in boldness and courage when you know that a peace that simply does not make sense to the world— God's peace—has set up a protective guard around your heart.

With God's peace to fortify you, helping you maintain healthy emotions in the midst of chaos, you have the potential to become extremely influential. You become the kind of person who can stand in the midst of the fire. You won't flinch when things get crazy around you. Your unbelieving friends will notice and be amazed. And they will want what you've got.

Of course, you can't experience this kind of peace if you run from adversity so fast that God never has an opportunity to prove himself. You need to remember that whatever trouble comes against you has passed through the powerful, yet permitting, hands of your Abba Father—Daddy—first. Loving fathers may allow their children to experience difficulty and hardship, but they will never allow them to be totally destroyed.

What makes this truth even more incredible is the fact that Jesus, who was God in a body, experienced everything you have ever felt or ever will feel—and more. He felt the pressure. He knew the sting of rejection. And yet he lived his entire life grounded in the peace of God.

Having such an all-powerful, all-knowing, always-present God for a heavenly Father is not something to be taken lightly. On the contrary, you can bank your very existence on God's promises and on your relationship with him. And in the midst of trouble, you can experience God's peace.

How does it affect you to know that Jesus experienced everything you have ever felt or ever will feel? How can you experience the same peace of God that Jesus did? Journal your thoughts here.

_____

_____

_____

_____

_____

_____

KNOWING WHAT TO EXPECT

EXP Several years ago we heard a story about a father who took his elementary-age son and daughter fishing on the Tombigbee Intercoastal Waterway in south Alabama. They had been fishing many times together, and the father had taught his children all the intricacies of fishing and boating safety. They had discussed many times what to do if trouble ever found them.

And on this day, trouble did.

As was their custom, the father and his children put their boat in at a landing and began to make their way out of the small tributary into the river. The Tombigbee Waterway is used by numerous industries for transporting products, so there are always huge barges and tugboats on the waterway. With the father sitting at the steering wheel and his son and daughter sitting behind him, they began to dodge the floating logs and trash as well as the other, much larger vessels.

Suddenly, in the wake of a passing barge, the boat began to rock. The father shouted over his shoulder for his kids to hold on. But the little boat was hardly a match for the pounding water; and the boat began to toss back and forth more violently, heavy logs and other trash in the waterway beating against its sides.

Finally, after what seemed like an eternity, they reached calmer waters. The father looked back to his right to make sure his son was OK. The boy was obviously shaken but fine. Then he turned and looked back to his left.

His little girl was not in the boat.

His eyes darted frantically to the water. There was his daughter's life vest, floating away—but his little girl was not in it. He began to scream her name, searching the muddy water for any sign of her. Nothing.

In the madness of the moment, it occurred to the father that if his little girl had been tossed out of the boat, she would have fallen into the water near the

PART ONE:
THE TRUTH ABOUT
INFLUENCE

outboard motor. In the split second that this thought ran through his mind, the motor suddenly shut off. The father's heart dropped: *She has fallen into the propeller*.

He rushed to the back of the boat and looked down into the water behind the motor, expecting to see a horrific sight of blood and torn flesh.

What he saw instead was his little girl's face—just below the surface of the water—smiling up at him. The sweatshirt she had been wearing was entangled in the prop, and she couldn't surface.

The father turned to his son to ask for a knife to cut the girl loose. His son was already there, holding the knife he wanted, knowingly extending it to him before he even asked. Quickly the father cut the sweatshirt away from the motor and pulled his daughter into the boat. For a long time, he held her and wept. Her sweatshirt was torn, but she did not have as much as a scratch.

When he finally regained his composure, the father asked his daughter how she could have been smiling when she was under the water in such a desperate situation.

"You taught us what to do in case of trouble," she responded. "I knew you would come and get me. I had nothing to be afraid of."

You, too, have nothing to be afraid of. Jesus has told you what to expect. And he's provided his peace to be a guard over your heart. This weekend memorize Philippians 4:4–9, which talks about the peace of God. Write the verses on a card and place it somewhere visible. Think about this question: Do you have the peace of God in your life? How can that peace make you influential?

KNOWING WHAT TO EXPECT

Understanding Influence
The Connection between Social Science
and the Gospel

He who thinks he leads,
but has no followers,
is only taking a walk.

JOHN MAXWELL

Understanding Influence
The Connection between Social Science and the Gospel

When U.S. Special Forces commandos attempted to rescue American prisoners from the infamous "Hanoi Hilton" prison during the Vietnam War, the operation was conducted almost without flaw. The commandos trained in great secrecy for weeks in advance. When the day finally came, the commando team quickly took control of the prison. The team was in and out and safely back at a U.S. base before enemy forces could respond.

Their only real flaw in the mission had to do with intelligence. Shortly before the raid, a remote-controlled drone was sent to collect information. During an in-flight turn, the drone banked slightly, causing its cameras to point toward the sky for a brief moment. As a result, the drone failed to capture imagery that would have revealed that the Hanoi Hilton prisoners had been moved. There were no prisoners to free.

Was the mission successful? It depends on how you define success. If the mission was to take control of the Hanoi Hilton, then the mission was successful. But if the mission was to free American prisoners, then the mission failed.[1]

In many ways this real-life story painfully corresponds with many of the church's efforts to reach teenagers with the truth about Jesus. Our array of programs, events, and environments is vast. Our means to free the "prisoners" are strategic, effective, and full of power.

But are we being successful? It depends on how you define success. If you define success by the number of bodies at youth group or the amount of pizza consumed at an outreach event, then maybe the answer is yes. But if you define success as individual teenage lives being impacted and changed forever through significant relationships with their Christian peers, then the mission is far from accomplished.

Let's establish a few things up front so there's no misunderstanding: God alone is the agent of change and the giver of life. Furthermore, God can and sometimes will bypass relationships to reach lost souls. Stories of his direct intervention in people's lives are both mind boggling and inspiring.

But that doesn't mean your role in reaching your lost friends is insignificant or unnecessary. What you can do within the scope of God's plan, you must do.

To be effective as a student of influence, you must not only recognize the role of God and his Spirit in reaching your lost friends, but also understand the principles that govern what makes those friends tick. You must understand how social science and the gospel connect. There are facts about human nature and the human psyche that are both predictable and powerful. They shouldn't be ignored. They're like the intelligence that was lacking at the Hanoi Hilton.

Do you have the "intelligence" you need to spiritually influence your friends for the sake of Christ?

Day
ONE

💬 Text

Read Matthew 15:17–19.

💬 Test

According to these verses, where do the words we speak originate from?
Where does our behavior originate from? _____

_____

_____

_____

Based upon your recent words and actions, what would you say is the condition of your heart right now? (Hint: Violence flows from an angry heart.
Sexual immorality flows from a lustful heart. Slander flows from a jealous
heart. You get the idea.) _____

_____

_____

_____

_____

_____

_____

_____

PART ONE:
THE TRUTH ABOUT
INFLUENCE

💬 Point

Any time you deliberately attempt to change another person's thoughts, feelings, or behavior—either through verbal or nonverbal communication—you
are exerting influence. And whether or not that person changes as a result of
your influence depends in large part upon his or her *attitude*.

An attitude is shaped when you hold up your own personal, internal "tape measure" and evaluate people, objects, concepts, and things against that scale, rating them from good to bad. Here, give it a try:

Atlanta Braves baseball: good or bad?

Squeezing toothpaste from the middle of the tube: good or bad?

Saddam Hussein: good or bad?

God: good or bad?

Your evaluation of these topics reveals your attitude or heart about them, which in turn provides your behavior with fuel for its fire. It keeps you moving in a certain direction. It is why you do what you do. Your heart determines your actions.

Now transfer this concept to the teenagers you know. Each of them has a picture of God—who they think he is and what they think he's like. They have evaluated him against their personal tape measure, formulating a particular attitude that now drives how they act in relation to him. If they have a picture of a God who is small or nonexistent, then their attitude probably drives them to be ambivalent or even antagonistic toward him. If they have a picture of a God who is huge and powerful and loving, then their attitude drives them to live a life of passion for Christ.

Christianity is about a change of heart.

As someone who has a picture of a big God, your objective is to influence the attitudes of those teenagers who have a picture of a small or nonexistent God. It's to persuade them to change their evaluation. The goal is heart change, because the heart drives behavior. Christianity, ultimately, isn't about behavior modification; it's about a change of heart. That's the point Jesus was trying to make in Matthew 15:17–19.

UNDERSTANDING INFLUENCE

Many Christian students (and youth leaders) have a tendency to focus their energies on changing a lost teenager's behavior. But you can't decide that a particular friend is in need of influence based on your judgment of his or her behavior. The heart is the real issue.

To affect behavior you have to affect the heart. It must be the object of your influence.

What are some of the ways you might influence the heart of a lost friend? Record your thoughts here.

_____

_____

_____

_____

_____

_____

_____

_____

_____

_____

_____

_____

_____

_____

_____

_____

_____

PART ONE:
THE TRUTH ABOUT
INFLUENCE

💬 Text

Read John 1:14.

💬 Test

What do you think is the significance of God becoming flesh?

_____

_____

_____

_____

What did the disciples experience as a result of God becoming a man?

_____

_____

_____

_____

What do you think John means when he talks about "his glory"?

_____

_____

_____

_____

💬 Point

God is the only agent of true change of the heart. But there are a lot of different ways that you can work with God as he accomplishes what only he can do in the hearts of your lost friends.

One thing you can do is help make a particular attitude *available*. Social scientists say that an attitude is available when you can think of it, when you're

UNDERSTANDING INFLUENCE

aware that you have a particular attitude on a topic, and when that attitude is turned on, so to speak.

You can actually increase the likelihood that someone will have a desired attitude available and turned on by doing what scientists call *priming*.

> **You "prime" your unbelieving friends by giving them a picture of the living God.**

Essentially, priming is a setup activity. You do something that gets the other person fired up or poised to think about a particular topic in a certain way.

If you want to be influential in the lives of your unbelieving friends, you have to "prime" them by giving them a living picture of who God is and the difference he can make in their lives. This means living a life characterized by passion for Christ and compassion for your lost friends—in close enough proximity for them to see the picture. Then when God prompts them to make a judgment about his son, Jesus Christ, the right primed attitude will be available to guide their behavior and drive how they respond.

If you've ever lived in the country and had to depend on a well for running water, you probably know about priming the pump. These days the pumps on most wells are motorized and run on electricity. But that doesn't mean they're trouble free. Invariably, the pump stops working at some inconvenient time, and you have to go out and prime the pump.

Growing up, Stuart often had to take a gallon milk jug full of water out to his family's pump and pour the water into a certain spot, in hopes that the pump would remember what to do, kick back on, and start pumping water again from the well. He would have to make trip after trip with his gallon jug of water to prime the pump. It was a time-consuming and painstaking process. Basically what he was doing was painting a "picture" to the pump—

so that the pump would develop an "attitude" about pumping water—so that it might develop a "behavior" of pumping water from the well.

In many ways that's what you must do: prime the heart pumps of your lost friends. You must get close enough to pour "living water" into their lives, encouraging them to develop a positive attitude toward the water so they'll begin to want it for themselves. You must give your friends an accurate picture of God to replace the faulty pictures that have influenced their attitudes and driven their behaviors up to now.

After all, isn't that why God came to earth and existed in a body: to prime mankind's pump by demonstrating in the flesh what God is like?

What attitudes do your lost friends have toward Jesus? What can you do to begin to "prime" their hearts so they'll be open and available to God? Journal your thoughts.

Day THREE

💬 Text

Read 1 Peter 2:11–12.

💬 Test

What does Peter say about our citizenship in the world? _____

_____

_____

_____

How are we supposed to live? What will be the result? _____

_____

_____

_____

💬 Point

Has this ever happened to you? You are walking down the street when you notice just ahead of you three or four people standing on the street corner, looking straight up in the air. As you move in closer to them, what do you do? You look up in the air. Is it a bird? Is it a plane? Is it Superman?

No, it's the principle of comparison. When other people are doing something, we think we should be doing it too. We compare our behavior against the standard of what everybody else is doing; and if we notice a discrepancy between our actions and what we observe in others, we change.

You can capitalize on this principle of influence. How? By living a life that presents your friends with an obviously different alternative to the lives being lived by most other teenagers. Think about it. How does your life compare to the students around you? What distinguishes you from other students? Is

**PART ONE:
THE TRUTH ABOUT
INFLUENCE**

there any noticeable difference—something that could cause an unbelieving teenager to compare his or her life to yours?

When Peter penned the passage in our Q Text, he was writing from Babylon, a major center for paganism. His goal was to encourage Christians to live in a way that would allow the unbelievers around them to see their "good deeds and glorify God on the day he visits us."

The Greek word used in verse 12 for *see* means "careful watching over a period of time." The fact is, if you live your life in a way that is consistently characterized by good words and deeds, prompted by your love for God and your compassion for people, your lost friends will take notice. They will recognize that your life is different from the lives of the other teenagers they hang around with. And they will know that the difference has something to do with the fact that you have God in your life.

Then—just maybe—those lost friends who've been observing your life over time will begin to evaluate their own lives in comparison to yours and make the choice to ask God into their lives too. Their decision won't be a snap judgment, but rather an educated one based on the influence of your life.

Who are the teenagers watching your life right now? What difference do they see when they compare your life to the lives of their other friends (and to their own)? Journal your thoughts.

_____

_____

_____

_____

_____

_____

_____

UNDERSTANDING INFLUENCE

Day FOUR

💬 Text

Read 1 John 3:18 and Galatians 5:6.

💬 Test

How does John say we are to love? _____

_____

_____

_____

Why do you think that love is the best expression of faith? _____

_____

_____

_____

_____

_____

💬 Point

**PART ONE:
THE TRUTH ABOUT
INFLUENCE**

Let's say you're walking down the street, minding your own business, when a stranger approaches from the opposite direction. The stranger makes eye contact with you and smiles. If you are like most people, you will automatically respond with a smile of your own as you pass the stranger and continue down the street.

A stranger gives you something (a smile) and you give back something in return (a smile). A nice way to meet people, but what does this have to do with influence?

Simple. We have a tendency to think that if someone gives us something and we accept it, we are now obligated to give something back. That's the principle behind the infamous youth-ministry pizza blasts. Students are enticed to come and chow down on all the free pizza they can eat. Then, once they've had their fill, they're asked to sit and listen to a speaker talk about the gospel. In other words: "We gave you something; now you give us something back."

The principle of reciprocity can be an effective influence tool. But when it comes to spiritual influence, expecting a reciprocal return on a relational investment can be a dangerous tactic. If you're not careful, it can backfire. In fact, churches and ministries over the years have so abused this principle that many unbelievers simply don't trust Christians anymore.

Recently a friend of ours had a conversation that illustrates the negative impact of reciprocity abuse. He was in Los Angeles, accompanying a group of guys who feed homeless people out of the back of a car one Sunday a month. Our friend noticed that this particular area of the city was dotted with churches and Christian shelters.

Unconditional love is like a giant heart magnet.

"Why don't the homeless people go to the churches and shelters for help?" he asked.

"Oh, no," one of the guys responded. "They won't set foot in the churches and shelters. There are always strings attached."

To be a student of influence, you must learn to love your lost friends with no expectation of reciprocity—no strings attached. Unconditional love is like a giant heart magnet. God tells us, "I have loved you with an everlasting love; I have drawn you with loving-kindness" (Jeremiah 31:3). Paul says that "God's kindness leads you toward repentance" (Romans 2:4). A heart simply can't resist true kindness and unconditional love. It's virtually impossible.

If you love your friends unconditionally, you will use the leverage of

UNDERSTANDING INFLUENCE

reciprocity without abusing it. And you will gain a degree of influence among your peers that will stand the test of time and pressure.

Do you love your unbelieving friends unconditionally? Or are there strings attached to some of your relationships? Be honest and write down what's in your heart.

_____

_____

_____

_____

_____

_____

_____

_____

_____

_____

_____

_____

_____

_____

_____

_____

_____

_____

_____

PART ONE:
THE TRUTH ABOUT
INFLUENCE

Day
FIVE

💬 Text

Read Matthew 6:22–23.

💬 Test

Why are your eyes important? _____

_____

_____

_____

_____

What do your eyes have to do with your ability to influence others? _____

_____

_____

_____

_____

_____

💬 Point

What's the dominant way people acquire new ideas and behaviors? By watching what other people do and then modeling them.

Think of a typical church service, for example. Most people in the service know what to do and when to do it; they know what not to do and when not to do it. Anyone who doesn't know the drill sticks out like a sore thumb. It usually doesn't take long for the newcomer to start imitating everyone else's example.

Modeling has two drawbacks, however. The first is that different people interpret what is being modeled in different ways. Let's say the class clown gets thrown out of the science lab and sent to the office for setting fire to a

UNDERSTANDING INFLUENCE

dissected frog. From this model some students learn that bad behavior gets punished and ought to be avoided. Other students learn that the best way to get out of a science lab is to act up in class. Others learn that as long as they don't set fire to the frogs, they can get away with almost anything else.

The second drawback is that people can look to the wrong things for their models. Some of your friends have seen and focused on the wrong stuff and the wrong people for so long that they have lost their perception of what is right. They have damaged their sensitivity to truth. Sensitivity to truth, like sensitivity to light, deteriorates gradually, almost imperceptibly.

At one point the truth was probably much more tangible and clear. Now it's not. No cheating on tests used to be a standard—but your friends have seen other students do it over and over again, make good grades, and not get caught. Obeying Mom and Dad used to be important—but they've seen many of their peers rebel against their parents' authority, have a blast every weekend, and never get grounded. Sex before marriage used to be a no-no—but they know teenagers who keep doing it, and no one's pregnant (yet). Now sex is no big deal.

> **Talk is cheap. What you need is relational leverage.**

PART ONE:
THE TRUTH ABOUT
INFLUENCE

Can you see why it's important for you to be a visible and viable influence in the lives of your unbelieving friends? Modeling is the most effective method you have for influencing their thinking and behavior. Talk is cheap. What you need is relational leverage. Modeling helps you gain crucial ground.

But jumping up and down on the lunch table and screaming, "Look at me!" is not the ticket. Neither is showing up only when trouble is in the air. No, the thing that will get you noticed is this: a consistent, compassionate, and godly life lived out before your friends day after day after day.

What are some of the ways you can begin to model the Christ-life before your unbelieving friends? Write your ideas here.

_____

_____

_____

_____

_____

_____

_____

_____

_____

_____

_____

_____

_____

_____

_____

_____

_____

_____

_____

_____

_____

_____

UNDERSTANDING INFLUENCE

EXP If you have a dog and you feed it canned food, what happens every evening when you hit the can opener? The animal comes running, even if you are opening a can of green beans. The dog has associated the sound of the opener with its food and has been conditioned to respond that way.

Conditioning works with people too. Back in K-Mart's heyday, there used to be a "phenomenon" called the *blue-light special.* Cost-conscious shoppers would make a beeline to the blue-light table because they associated the light with a good sale. Research proved that people were more likely to buy the sale item under the blue light, even if the item wasn't really a good value.

Conditioning takes place in all kinds of arenas. Our culture has even been conditioned to respond in certain ways to Christianity and the church. The aftermath of the terrorist attacks on September 11 was a conditioned response to the very best of what the church ought to be. People flocked to churches to find solace, peace, and hope. Interestingly, they evacuated the churches almost as quickly as they invaded them. Why? Did the emotion of the horror of those events wear off? We doubt it. Maybe the answer lies in what they found—or didn't find—when they got there.

PART ONE:
THE TRUTH ABOUT
INFLUENCE

How your lost friends see you and respond to you can be a matter of conditioning. Think about it: Are you the first person your lost friends run to when trouble or tragedy strikes? When their lives are turned upside down, do they think of you as the one friend they know they can confide in, ask advice of, and count on?

Consider the numerous stories in the Gospels of people who, in the direst of situations, sought Jesus out. Why did the Roman officer come looking for Jesus when his servant was dying? Why did lepers and paralytics seek him? Because, in many ways, Jesus had conditioned them to do so. The life he lived day after day in their midst had convinced them that he was accepting, compassionate, available, and capable of offering help that no one else could.

Right now you are conditioning your unbelieving friends to think of you in a particular way. And you are conditioning them to think of God—the one you say that you serve—in a particular way. In effect, you are modeling a picture of God. Is it a huge masterpiece, like the ceiling of Michelangelo's Sistine Chapel in Rome, which one cannot pass without stopping and considering? Or is it a fuzzy Polaroid worth no more than a quick glance and all too easily tossed aside?

This weekend, get out some of your old yearbooks or class photos and ask yourself, "What do I think about when I see pictures of some of my old friends and classmates? What do they probably think about when they see pictures of me?" What are some of the ways you can improve your "picture" in your friends' minds and become a greater influence for Christ in their lives?

UNDERSTANDING INFLUENCE

The Principles

Scientists at NASA built a gun specifically to launch dead chickens at the windshields of airliners, military jets, and space shuttles traveling at maximum velocity. The idea was to simulate the frequent collisions that occur with airborne fowl and test the strength of the vehicles' windshields. When British engineers heard about the gun, they were eager to test it on the windshields of their new high-speed trains. Arrangements were made, and a gun was sent across the Atlantic.

In the first simulation, the British engineers watched in shock as the chicken hurled out of the barrel of the gun, crashed into the supposedly shatterproof windshield, smashed it to smithereens, blasted through the control console, snapped the engineer's backrest in two, and embedded itself in the back wall of the cabin—like an arrow shot from a bow.

The horrified Brits sent NASA the disastrous results of the experiment, along with the designs of the windshield. They begged the U.S. scientists for suggestions.

NASA responded with a one-line memo:

"Defrost the chicken."[1]

The principles that follow are the "frozen chickens" of becoming a student of influence. They are the principles you need to embrace in order to have influence and leverage with your unbelieving friends. They're what you need to "break through."

Don't defrost.

Principle

You must develop, be able to verbally articulate,
and live by personal standards.

Critical Question

Are you developing and living by standards
that you can clearly articulate to others?

Key Passage

1 Peter 2:11–12

PRINCIPLE 1

The Standards Principle
Gaining the High Ground

**If you don't stand for something,
you will fall for anything.**

AUTHOR UNKNOWN

The Standards Principle
Gaining the High Ground

On one of the walls in our offices is a photograph of the Gettysburg National Military Park in Gettysburg, Pennsylvania. The picture shows Little Round Top, which was the highest elevation on that old Civil War battlefield. As any military strategist will tell you, the army that has the high ground has the advantage. If you can control the high ground, you can control the outcome of the battle. Apparently at a very critical point in the Battle of Gettysburg, both the Union and Confederate armies realized simultaneously that neither army occupied Little Round Top. Regiments from both armies literally raced on foot from opposite sides to the top. The outcome of perhaps the most consequential battle in the Civil War was decided because the Union army beat the Confederate army to the high ground!

You can use that picture and its story as a reminder: Your battle is not just to hold certain beliefs. It is not to maintain your "safe" position. It is to capture the high ground. Your battle is to live a life of conviction that reflects the overwhelming passion God has for you and you have for him—and that reflects his passion and yours for the lost people around you.

Down through the centuries, armies have always gone to war carrying a banner, or standard. They have rallied around their standard, fought for it, even died for it. Scenes of Denzel Washington in *Glory* or Mel Gibson in *The Patriot* come to mind. In these and similar movies, intense fighting is always the backdrop as the standard is lifted and waved in slow motion. The raising of the standard acts like a summons, calling all those who would rise up and fight to join the battle—sometimes against overwhelming odds.

God is looking for teenagers who are willing to hold uncompromisingly to their standards. He is looking for teenagers who are not afraid to raise and wave those standards high. He is looking for students who are ready and willing to race to the high ground.

Will you be one of those students?

Day
ONE

⬚ Text

Read Ephesians 5:3–4 and 8–12.

⬚ Test

Do you have a "hint" in your life of any of the things Paul mentions? Which ones?_____

_____

_____

_____

_____

How is darkness exposed? What does this passage tell you about how you can expose darkness without offending or judging your lost friends?

_____

_____

_____

_____

_____

_____

_____

_____

PART TWO:
THE PRINCIPLES

⬚ Point

As a Christian student, you need to have certain specific, God-based standards that distinguish you from your peers. And these standards must be non-negotiable. The space shuttle will literally self-destruct at Max Q if the substance of the vehicle is the least bit weakened or compromised. You will self-destruct under pressure, too, if you compromise your standards.

A standard is a rule. It's like a fence for a dog. It keeps him in the yard to play to his heart's content, but it also keeps him out of the street. Of course, a standard restricts freedom in a sense, and nobody likes that. Not even God. In the perfect world of Eden, God gave Adam and Eve 99 percent freedom and only 1 percent rule. God definitely prefers freedom to rules.

So why does a God who loves freedom so much make so many rules to restrict it? you may wonder.

Here's the answer: In this world there are activities that, once partaken of, restrict freedom. And since God is all for freedom, he doesn't want you to be involved in anything that will restrict it. Think of it this way. To be free to smoke is to lose a host of greater freedoms. Ask any man or woman who is dying of lung cancer which freedom they would prefer—the freedom to smoke, or the freedom to live? The freedom to smell good, or the freedom to smell like an ashtray twenty-four hours a day?

For you to be free to put anything you want into your mind sacrifices your freedom to control your thoughts and perspectives on sex, parents, authority figures, and life in general. To be free to fool around with sex as much as you want sacrifices your freedom to one day enjoy a marriage partner to the maximum. It sacrifices your freedom from guilt and shame.

Who is more free: a teenager with a baby or a teenager without? A teenager with a drinking problem or a teenager without? A teenager with an education or a teenager without?

Adam and Eve decided to do things their own way for the sake of freedom. They thought they would gain freedom by disregarding the standard God set. Instead they lost freedom—and a whole lot more.

When you choose to live by godly standards, you aren't losing your freedom; you're protecting it. Maximum freedom is always found under God's authority. Think of an umbrella. When a deluge hits, you're protected from

THE STANDARDS PRINCIPLE

the elements as long as you stay under the umbrella. The second you decide to step out from under that protection, however, you get wet. In a similar way, the moment you step out from under the umbrella of the authority of God's Word, you put yourself at risk for dire consequences.

Be honest. What godly standards are missing from your life? What freedoms have you put in jeopardy as a result? Journal your thoughts.

Day TWO

🗩 Text

Read 1 Timothy 4:8.

🗩 Test

How does physical training parallel spiritual training? _____

_____

_____

_____

_____

_____

What are the benefits of godliness? _____

_____

_____

_____

_____

_____

_____

🗩 Point

This may seem counterintuitive, but having unbelieving friends can actually help you grow spiritually. In fact, if you feel as if you've had a "lid" on your spiritual growth lately, the culprit may be a lack of friendships with unbelievers. You're not being spiritually challenged by lost friends who think and believe differently than you do. As Bill Walton, former UCLA and NBA basketball great, commented recently on TV, "If everyone is thinking the same, no one is thinking."

THE STANDARDS PRINCIPLE

The dynamics of weightlifting apply here. Muscle growth occurs when resistance is met. You can't build physical muscles without resistance. And you can't build spiritual muscles without the same. Having friends who question your faith is as healthy for you as it is for them. Responding to queries of who, what, why, and how requires you to dig for answers that go deeper than "Because my youth leader said so" or "Because I read it in the Bible." A challenged faith becomes a strong faith.

There's another dynamic at work too: You naturally intensify your efforts at spiritual growth when you know your peers are watching you. We all perform better when someone is watching, don't we? It's a fact of life. A basketball player's intensity and focus increase when the girl of his dreams walks into the gym and sits in the stands. You work harder on your homework when your mom, dad, or teacher looks over your shoulder. And we all jog faster and with better form when cars are coming as opposed to when we're all alone on the road. Some of the greatest times of spiritual growth you will ever experience will come when you know you have friends who are lost, intently watching your life.

> **You naturally intensify your efforts at spiritual growth when you know your peers are watching you.**

If you don't have unbelieving friends watching you, however, you are at risk for becoming spiritually lazy. You're like a soldier who never goes to war. A soccer player with no game to play. We've seen students become so bored with their unchallenged faith that they start looking around for something, *anything,* to spark their interest. They're the ones who get caught up in tangents—striving to become *Purpose Driven Youth* while *Fishing the Planet* as they apply *The Seven Checkpoints,* pray *The Prayer of Jabez for Sixteen Year Olds,* and sing songs from the latest Passion CD at See You at the Pole. They're awfully busy. But spiritually, they're getting nowhere.

How are your spiritual muscles? What can you do to make those muscles stronger? Journal your thoughts.

THE STANDARDS PRINCIPLE

Day THREE

💬 Text

Read 1 Timothy 4:12.

💬 Test

In what areas was Timothy to set an example for others? _____

_____

_____

_____

Do you think your age negates your ability to be influential? Why or why not? _____

_____

_____

_____

_____

_____

_____

_____

**PART TWO:
THE PRINCIPLES**

💬 Point

When someone says the word *ghetto*, what comes to your mind? A specific geographical area? By definition a ghetto is simply a subculture. And all subcultures have distinctives that "brand" them—their own kinds of music, language, and fashion sense, for example. Anyone who is not indoctrinated and familiar with a specific subculture feels alienated and disconnected within that subculture. They feel out of balance in the midst of it.

Christianity and youth ministry, in particular, have become a ghetto, of sorts. We have our own language. (When we speak Christian-ese, most people have no clue what we're talking about.) We have our own clothing. (You can probably go to your dresser right now and pull out at least one camp T-shirt with a scripture reference on it.) We have our own television shows, radio stations, and bookstores. We have our own music—we even have our own boy bands.

The problem is, you can get so indoctrinated into this "youth group" sub-culture that you are unable to connect relationally with anyone outside of it. You feel out of balance whenever you're outside the four walls of the church.

Basically you have three alternatives:

1. You can surround yourself with Christians and eventually become a lazy, unbalanced, spiritually bored rabbit chaser.

2. You can immerse yourself in the "lost world" lifestyle and let your lost friends lead you to destruction.

3. You can commit yourself to making an impact in your sphere of influence by developing balanced friendships with unbelievers according to God's guidelines.

Let's be very clear. There is a razor-thin line between influencing others and being influenced. Yesterday we said that having lost friends can help you grow spiritually. But the opposite is also true. Non-Christian friends can be devastating to your spiritual growth. Sometimes getting away from a lost friend is the best thing that can happen to you spiritually.

The truth is, if you develop friendships with unbelievers but ignore God's guidelines for those friendships, you *will* go down. If you learn to develop balanced friendships according to God's principles, however, you can build effective relational bridges and become influential in your friends' lives.

This leads us to the first principle of becoming a student of influence:

THE STANDARDS PRINCIPLE

In order to be an influence without being influenced, you must develop, be able to articulate, and live by personal standards.

In other words, you must learn how to derive and arrive at convictions that become standards in critical areas of your life. Then you must learn how to live out your standards in the circumstances of your day-to-day life. Finally, you must learn how to articulate those standards simply, clearly, and with confidence. A standard not applied is no standard at all.

What example are you setting for others in the areas of speech, life, love, faith, and purity? What standards do you need to develop in these areas? Write them down here.

_____

_____

_____

_____

_____

_____

_____

_____

_____

_____

_____

_____

_____

_____

PART TWO:
THE PRINCIPLES

Day
FOUR

⊛ Text

Read John 3:1–21.

⊛ Test

Why do you think Nicodemus went to speak with Jesus?_____

_____

_____

_____

_____

What qualities did Jesus possess that caused Nicodemus to gravitate toward him? _____

_____

_____

_____

⊛ Point

Your standards are what will set you apart in the minds of your unbelieving friends. Standards are the separation factor. And they are the primary tool God will use to get the attention of your unbelieving peers. They're the catalyst that will prompt your lost friends to finally get around to asking the question you've been dying for them to ask: "Why?"

"Why did you leave the party?"

"Why won't you try it?"

"Why are you always so nice to that person?"

And just like a raised hand in class, an unbelieving friend's *why* gives you permission to speak truth into his or her life.

THE STANDARDS PRINCIPLE

Unfortunately many Christian students have been conditioned to answer questions that, quite frankly, their lost friends aren't asking. To knock on a stranger's door and present an answer to an unasked question is kind of presumptuous, isn't it? Have you ever been around someone who continuously gives you his or her unsolicited opinion on everything under the sun? What do you do with people like that? I know what I do. I get away from them. They start to irritate me.

As a student of influence, your job is to "always be prepared to give an answer to everyone who asks you to give the reason for the hope that you have" (1 Peter 3:15). Not prepared to answer questions that aren't being asked. But prepared because you've earned the right to be heard; and then, prepared to articulate truth in a clear and simple way that engages the heart of your unbelieving friend.

> **It's time to put up or shut up.**

Answering the why question can be one of the most frightening steps of faith you will ever take. All of us have felt that knot in our stomach when we realize that the moment is now. Time to put up or shut up. You can fade at this point, mainly out of concern for what your friends will think of you. But the truth is, the majority of the teenagers who put you down or ridicule you for your standards once held those same standards but compromised. Who, then, has the right to be critical? What would you rather be guilty of: consistency or compromise?

If your lost friends have never asked you the why question, you need to consider two possible explanations. First, it may be that your friends simply need more time to come around. Or second, it may be that your standards— the catalyst for the why question—are weak or nonexistent.

**PART TWO:
THE PRINCIPLES**

When was the last time someone asked you the why question? What does that say about your standards? Journal your thoughts.

Day FIVE

💬 Text

Read Psalm 119:11.

💬 Test

How do you think David "hid" God's word in his heart? _____

_____

_____

_____

_____

Why is hiding God's word in your heart so important? _____

_____

_____

_____

_____

_____

💬 Point

**PART TWO:
THE PRINCIPLES**

How do you develop strong and consistent standards? We have crystallized the process of developing a standard into an easy-to-remember formula:

Biblical Principle or Command + Wisdom = Standard

Most teenagers think the Bible is nothing more than a rule book. And of course, Scripture is full of imperatives, or commands, from God. (You're familiar with the Ten Commandments . . . ?) But the truth is, Scripture gives us many more _principles_ than it does _commands_.

Principles involve cause and effect: If you do this, then that will happen.

One way to understand the difference is to think of road signs. Let's say you're driving home and you see a sign that says Speed Limit 55 MPH. That's a command. It's the law. (Some of us forget to obey it sometimes—but we won't go there.)

Later on that same road, you come to a curve that is marked with several yellow signs with black arrows indicating a sharp left turn. Just preceding the arrow signs is another sign that says Slow Down. Now, there is no law that says you must slow down to a certain speed and curve left. But if you don't slow down and curve left, you may quickly find that you no longer exist. (And if you are on the road to Stuart's house, you will wind up airborne and landing in a pond!)

The speed-limit sign is like a command. The Slow Down and arrow signs are more like principles.

To develop a standard, you begin with a command or principle. Then you add the second key ingredient, which is wisdom. Wisdom itself is a combination of two things: knowledge plus action. It's not enough to have one without the other. Think about it. If you have all the Bible knowledge in the world but never use it in a way that impacts others for Christ, what good is it? If you are full of zeal for God, always ready for action, but have no idea how to answer the why question when it's asked, what's the benefit?

Scripture warns against becoming imbalanced. James challenges, "Do not merely listen to the word, and so deceive yourselves. Do what it says" (James 1:22). In other words, knowledge without active obedience is deceptive and foolish. At the same time, Solomon says, "It is not good to have zeal without knowledge, nor to be hasty and miss the way" (Proverbs 19:2). In effect, to act without knowledge is equally foolish. True biblical wisdom is the melding of knowledge and action together.

THE STANDARDS PRINCIPLE

To become a student of influence, you must learn to apply wisdom to the commands and principles of God. Then you can begin to develop the kinds of strong, godly standards necessary to impact your lost friends for Christ.

Spend some time writing down the standards you have set (or want to set, starting today) in your life. What are these standards based on? How can they enhance your influence with your lost friends?

_____

_____

_____

_____

_____

_____

_____

_____

_____

_____

_____

_____

_____

_____

_____

_____

_____

_____

_____

_____

_____

PART TWO:
THE PRINCIPLES

EXP If you're going to interact on a regular basis with teenagers who believe, think, talk, and live differently from you, then you must have standards. Why? Because God doesn't want you to be taken prisoner by the consequences of bad choices. He also wants to use your standards as a catalyst to get the attention of your lost friends.

Many teenagers ask us, "Exactly how many standards do I need to set?" (Translation: "What's the least amount I can get away with?") Here's the answer we give: The more dangerous the environment, the more rules you need.

It's important to set standards ahead of time—*before* you find yourself in a dangerous or tempting situation. An on-the-spot decision made in a peer-pressured environment is almost always the wrong decision. That's why we're going to spend next week developing and solidifying the standards principle in five key areas: friendship, dating and sex, entertainment, drinking, and parties.

This weekend ask yourself: "Do I have standards in any of these areas? Can I articulate them? Am I living them out?" Pray for God to prepare your heart and mind for the important work you'll begin on Monday.

THE STANDARDS PRINCIPLE

PRINCIPLE 1, CONTINUED

Applying the Standards Principle
Developing Standards in Five Key Areas

There's no substitute for personal experience
when it comes to dealing with problems.
That's particularly true in times of crisis,
when there's less time to develop ideas and plans.
Wisdom gained from one's own history
provides a head start.

RUDOLPH GIULIANI

Applying the Standards Principle
Developing Standards in Five Key Areas

When it comes to helping students develop wisdom, youth leaders and parents have a hard time balancing their natural desire to protect "their kids," to keep them morally and physically safe, versus their teenagers' need to have the freedom to fail. Failure is a critical component of success. We don't like it, and we have tried to excise it from our homes and ministries; but the truth is, failure is one of life's greatest teachers.

Think about it. You actually learn very little from your successes. Most of the invaluable lessons of life come from your failures. That's why books written by successful people who failed and learned from their mistakes make the bestseller list. Experience breeds wisdom.

This is a pivotal week in your journey to become a student of influence. Because the Standards Principle is so important, we are spending two weeks on it. We have set up this second week differently from the weeks you have already completed and the weeks that will follow. Instead of having a Q Text, a Q Test, and a Q Point, we have sections designed to walk you through the Standard Formula we introduced in Week Four:

Biblical Principle or Command + Wisdom = Standard

For the next five days, we want to help you develop standards in five crucial areas of your life: dating and sex, entertainment, drinking, friendships, and parties. Certainly there are other areas where standards are needed. But these five are a good start. Once you learn to apply the Standard Formula in these five areas, you will be equipped to apply it in other areas as well.

As you work through the next five days, you may find that you struggle to properly understand and put into practice the commands and principles found in God's Word. A standard built on faulty theology or opinion will buckle under pressure. Or you may find that you struggle with the wisdom part of the equation. Deciding the wise thing to do can be hard if you lack experience or knowledge in a particular area. This is where your parents and youth leaders can help. Don't hesitate to go to them for guidance in discerning what God says about a certain subject.

Remember your goal: to be an influence without being influenced. To be the influence-er, not the influence-ee. To reach this goal, it's imperative that you face and work through some hard questions about God's truth, your own heart, and the wisdom needed to establish standards in critical areas of your life.

Are you ready to dive in?

Day ONE

Developing a Standard for Dating and Sex

Biblical Commands and Principles

Read these verses and record what they imply about dating and sex:

2 Corinthians 6:14 _____

_____

1 Corinthians 6:18–20 _____

_____

1 Corinthians 7:39 _____

_____

1 Thessalonians 4:3–8 _____

_____

Proverbs 18:22 _____

_____

Wisdom Notes

PART TWO:
THE PRINCIPLES

This may be the toughest area in which to set standards and then live by them. When hormones get cranked up, standards for dating and sex often fall to half-mast. Many Christian students who've lost their testimony with their unbelieving friends have done so in this context.

There are two groups of students in this area: those who have had sex and those who have not. Those who have think it's too late to develop standards. Those who haven't think they don't need standards. Both are wrong.

The probability is about 100 percent that you will be tempted in the area of sex. And at that moment, having sex may seem like the right thing to do. That's why you must decide *now* how far you will go and then draw that line.

The higher you set your standard, the less danger you'll be in if, in a moment of insanity, you mess up and lower it. For example, let's say Chip's sex and dating standard is holding hands only, no kissing. But one night in a moment of passion, while watching an Adam Sandler movie, he breaks his rule. What has he done? He has kissed a girl. The consequences will be minimal (unless she has bad breath and a canker sore).

But what if Chip's standard is that he will engage in petting but not intercourse, and one night, in a moment of passion, he breaks his rule? What has he done? He has had intercourse, and the consequences are more than significant. They may have lifelong implications.

You only have to look around you to know that sex outside of marriage messes people up. It destroys futures, relationships, trust, intimacy, and self-esteem, to name only a few things. God's commands and principles about dating and sex aren't meant to confine you; they're meant to keep you free.

Take some time to challenge yourself with these hard questions:

- How far do you want your next boyfriend or girlfriend to have gone with his or her previous date?

- Which story do you want to tell to the person you marry one day: "I waited for you"; "I blew it at sixteen, but I made up my mind after that to wait for you"; or "I blew it and decided what the heck . . . "? Which story do you want to hear?

- What kind of person should you date? Is dating only people who say they are Christians narrow enough? What are the characteristics you are looking for in a future spouse?

- What are you going to do when your friend wants to fix you up with his or her sibling or best friend? Are you willing to appear snobbish? Are you willing to be misunderstood?

APPLYING THE STANDARDS PRINCIPLE

By setting high standards in the area of dating and sex, you protect yourself. You protect your testimony. And you blow your unbelieving friends' minds. If you can resist sex, something *must* be different about you! You reveal an inner strength that your friends cannot deny or ignore.

Standard

Adding the commands and principles of God's Word to the wisdom you have gained, what should your standard be for dating and sex? Write it out and then journal your thoughts.

Developing a Standard for Entertainment

Biblical Commands and Principles

Read these verses and record what they imply about entertainment:

Ephesians 5:3–12 _____

_____

Romans 8:6_____

_____

Romans 7:22–23_____

_____

Romans 12:2_____

_____

1 Peter 4:7 _____

_____

Colossians 3:1–8_____

_____

Philippians 4:8_____

_____

Matthew 15:18–19_____

_____

Wisdom Notes

If you don't develop standards in the area of entertainment (music, movies, videos, magazines, and so on), you will eventually find yourself being entertained by sin. And as a Christian, you send a double message when you laugh at sin and then try to convince your unbelieving friends that they need to quit sinning.

You may think, *But won't my friends think I'm too good for them if I say I really don't want to see that movie?* Well, what's the alternative? Most teenagers detest hypocrisy almost as much as they do homework. Yet the alternative to having unbelieving friends think you are too good for them is having unbelieving friends think you are a hypocrite. Which is worse?

When presented with an entertainment choice, ask yourself hard questions such as:

- Does this CD glorify sin in its lyrics?

- Does this movie use sin to attempt to entertain me?

- What will I *not* watch or listen to?

- What specific areas in entertainment cause me to struggle?

Standard

Adding the commands and principles of God's Word to the wisdom you have gained, what should your standard be for entertainment? Write it out and then journal your thoughts.

Developing a Standard for Drinking

Biblical Commands and Principles

Read these verses and record what they imply about drinking alcohol.

Ephesians 5:18 _____

_____

1 Corinthians 8:9–13 _____

_____

1 Corinthians 10:23–33 _____

_____

Proverbs 20:1 _____

_____

Proverbs 23:29–35 _____

_____

Wisdom Notes

Any conversation about alcohol has to start at this point: If you are under the legal drinking age and you decide to drink, you are already violating a God-given standard. Romans 13:1 is very clear that Christians are to submit to the governing authorities that God has established. Consequently, to drink while under age is to rebel against authority and ultimately against God.

But let's be painfully realistic. Many students—even those who call themselves Christians—are not adhering to that standard. Despite laws against underage drinking and the selling of alcohol to minors; beer, wine, and other drinks are all too available to high-school students. And just as with sex, there are two camps: those who have partaken and those who have not. Those who have usually think it is too late to develop a standard. Those who

APPLYING THE STANDARDS PRINCIPLE

haven't usually think they don't need a standard. Both are wrong.

Generally speaking, teenagers drink because they have never set standards about where they will and will not go and whom they will and will not go with. They drink—even though they know they shouldn't—because they never decide not to. That's why you need to think through your attitude about drinking and come up with a rock-solid standard.

Virtually all teenagers who have never tasted alcohol will experience a real temptation to drink at some point. If you haven't yet, you probably will. At that moment it may not seem wrong; and if you don't have a standard, you will most likely give in. But as soon as you lift that can or cup to your lips, your ability to positively influence the students around you will begin to dissipate.

The fact is, your unbelieving friends expect you, as a Christian student, not to drink. When you do, your friends lose respect for you—along with all hope that Christ is real and can do something worthwhile in their lives. Whether you like it or not, alcohol is a dividing line in teenage America. Choosing not to drink sets you apart immediately.

**PART TWO:
THE PRINCIPLES**

If you have gone out drinking with your friends in the past and make a decision now to set a "no drinking" standard, expect a certain amount of rejection. Many of your so-called friends will show their true colors by choosing a liquid in a can over you. But at least you will have an opportunity to begin rebuilding a consistent testimony.

Sit down at home by yourself and write out a list of the pros and cons of drinking. At the bottom of the two columns, answer this question: "Will I be a more effective witness if I drink or if I don't drink?" We encourage you to make a decision about drinking now, when the pressure is not on and you're not in the middle of Max Q.

Standard

Adding the commands and principles of God's Word to the wisdom you have gained, what should your standard be for drinking? Write it out and then journal your thoughts.

Day FOUR

Developing a Standard for Friendship

Biblical Commands and Principles

Read these verses and record what they imply about friendship.

Proverbs 13:20 _____

_____

Proverbs 17:17 _____

_____

Proverbs 18:24 _____

_____

Proverbs 22:24–25 _____

_____

Proverbs 27:6 _____

_____

John 15:13_____

_____

Wisdom Notes

PART TWO:
THE PRINCIPLES

Your friends will determine the quality and direction of your life. This is a proven, unarguable fact. Many times your friends will have a greater influence on you than God, your parents—even your youth leaders. Clearly, your choice of friends is important! But that doesn't mean you must avoid all teenagers who don't believe the same things you do. How else will those teenagers be reached for Christ? You need to find that delicate balance that exists between avoiding unhealthy friendships and having the opportunity to influence your lost peers.

Ask yourself these hefty questions:

- What does a healthy friendship look like?

- Am I becoming a friend worth having?

- Do I have Christian friends who are concerned about my relationship with Christ and equally concerned about their own relationship with Christ?

- Do I have boundaries when it comes to friends who don't have a relationship with Christ? What should those boundaries be?

Standard

Adding the commands and principles of God's Word to the wisdom you have gained, what should your standard be for friendship? Write it out and then journal your thoughts.

APPLYING THE STANDARDS PRINCIPLE

Day FIVE

Developing a Standard for Parties

Biblical Commands and Principles

Read these verses and record what they imply about your attendance at parties.

Proverbs 13:20 _____

_____

Colossians 3:20 _____

_____

1 Corinthians 10:31–33 _____

_____

Proverbs 1:10 _____

_____

1 Thessalonians 5:5–8 _____

_____

Wisdom Notes

If you are making relational connections with your peers, your unbelieving friends are probably going to invite you to parties from time to time. You need to decide in advance what kinds of parties you will and will not go to. Most importantly you need to be willing and able to leave if the environment turns negative. In fact, if you don't possess the self-assurance and self-control to leave a party when things get out of hand, you are not mature enough to go to parties in the first place.

If you're not willing to leave . . . you're not mature enough to go.

Ask yourself these hard questions:

**PART TWO:
THE PRINCIPLES**

- Should I go to a party where everyone will be drinking, even if I choose not to drink?

- What about a party with no adult supervision?

- At what point will I leave a party, even if it means looking stupid?

- Could simply being present at a particular party damage my reputation? If people hear that I was there, what impact will that have on them?

Standard

Adding the commands and principles of God's Word to the wisdom you have gained, what should your standard be for parties? Write it out and then journal your thoughts.

_____

_____

_____

_____

_____

_____

_____

_____

_____

_____

_____

_____

APPLYING THE STANDARDS PRINCIPLE

EXP We have taught the principle of setting standards to students countless times, and it never fails that the same scene materializes. Many students are writing feverishly, asking questions, and interacting with each other. But one group of students simply sits and stares. They are nonresponsive and act uninterested.

So we conclude by asking them, "Do you have standards? We're not asking if you have preferences. Do you have things you are so convinced of that you refuse to compromise on them—regardless of who is asking, how old they are, how good looking they are, where you are, or who will know?" We then make note of the fact that while we were speaking, many of them didn't write even one thing down. It's not that we're legalistic jerks who demand that students take notes. Nor do we think our communication skills are so unbelievable that everyone should be writing down everything we say. We ask the question because we know that most of the students in the room have lost friends. And most of them really want to be influential in their friends' lives.

And then we ask them to lean in, listen close, and hear this well:

PART TWO:
THE PRINCIPLES

If you're unwilling to develop standards, then you're not mature enough to have relationships with people who are lost.

Without fail, all the air gets sucked out of the room at that point. Not because the students feel guilty for not taking notes, but because they realize they are living lives with no standards.

Do you have standards? Remember, Jesus Christ himself has given you the directive to go and make disciples. But if you're unwilling to develop and live by standards, then you aren't mature enough to have relationships with lost friends. And if you can't have relationships with lost friends, you can't make disciples. It's impossible. Who are you going to influence? The bottom line is this: If you refuse to develop standards, you are ultimately refusing to obey the Great Commission. You have put yourself in a position of disobeying Christ.

Strong words? Yes. But true? The answer is between you and God.

Spend this weekend thinking back on the standards you developed over the past five days. Then come up with at least one other area in your life in which you need to have a standard, and use the Standard Formula to develop and articulate it. Use a Bible concordance to find Scripture verses that apply. Talk to a parent or youth leader if you need help.

APPLYING THE STANDARDS PRINCIPLE

Principle

You must establish your own spiritual health as a priority over the spiritual health of the friends you are attempting to influence.

Critical Question

Are you prioritizing your relationship with Christ over your relationships with friends?

Key Passage

Matthew 6:33

PRINCIPLE 2

The Priorities Principle
Putting Your Own Spiritual Health First

When it comes to the whole subject
of loving others, you must know this:
How you handle your own heart
is how you will handle theirs.

JOHN ELDREDGE

The Priorities Principle
Putting Your Own Spiritual Health First

If you have ever flown the friendly skies, you've heard the canned flight-attendant spiel—you know, the one that goes, "In case of cabin depressurization, oxygen masks will drop from the overhead compartment . . ." Adult passengers are instructed that in case of an emergency, they are to place oxygen masks over their own mouths first before helping their children put on their masks.

Doesn't that sound almost cruel? Most parents' first instinct is to get those oxygen masks on their kids before taking care of themselves. But if they do that, they're making a mistake. If they pass out from oxygen deprivation, how will they be of any help to their sons and daughters? They can't take care of their kids if they're unable to function. In spite of their natural parental instinct to put their children first, the wisest thing to do in an emergency at 30,000 feet is to make their own physical welfare a priority over their kids'.

Counterintuitive? Yes. But so true.

If you are going to become a student who can be influential without being influenced—who can endure maximum dynamic pressure and still lead others to Christ—you must learn to do the same thing on a spiritual level: Put your own spiritual welfare before the spiritual welfare of others.

Mark it down. A time will come when you will find yourself being drawn into things you have no business getting involved in. When that happens, you will need to make your own spiritual growth a priority over the spiritual growth of your lost peers. You will need to make the decision to back off the relationship—or even bail out completely. Doing so will take courage. But your intimacy with your Creator will depend on it.

Your own spiritual health and growth must be top priority. Is there any relationship in your life that is more important to you than your relationship with Jesus?

Should there be?

Day
ONE

🗨 Text

Read John 6:1–15.

🗨 Test

After meeting the spiritual and physical needs of the people he was influencing, what did Jesus do? _____

_____

_____

_____

What do you think is the significance of Jesus choosing to go away from the crowds? _____

_____

_____

_____

🗨 Point

PART TWO:
THE PRINCIPLES

MaxQ

When it comes to applying the Priorities Principle, you have a good example to follow: Jesus. Throughout his life, Jesus put his own spiritual welfare ahead of the spiritual welfare of others.

Consider the feeding of the five thousand (more like twelve thousand when you add women and children) described in John 6:1–15. Jesus had a huge crowd eating out of the palm of his hand. They would have done anything he said—especially after seeing him turn two sardines and five loaves of Roman Meal nine grain into a seafood buffet at Red Lobster. They were ready to follow him anywhere. But what did Jesus do? He sensed that it was time for him to pray and get spiritually renewed, and he withdrew to a mountain to do so.

Or consider the temptation of Jesus in the desert. The Bible tells us that "the devil took him to a very high mountain and showed him all the kingdoms of the world and their splendor. 'All of this I will give you,' he said, 'if you will bow down and worship me.'

"Jesus said to him, 'Away from me, Satan!'" (Matthew 4:8–10).

Jesus chose obedience to God over having immediate influence over the world. He responded the way you need to respond when having influence with your friends would mean disobeying God. He opted for his own spiritual welfare—and so should you.

When you find yourself tempted to lower your standards or sacrifice your walk with God in order to stay in a relationship with an unbelieving friend, you need to make your own spiritual health the priority. Your situation is like being in a depressurized plane: You need to reach up, grab God's oxygen mask, and breathe deeply. You can't be any help to your lost peers if you're not spiritually strong yourself.

What priority do you place on having personal time alone with God? Why is that personal time important? Record your thoughts.

THE PRIORITIES PRINCIPLE

Day TWO

💬 Text

Read Matthew 5:13.

💬 Test

Why do you think Jesus compared his followers to salt? _____

_____

_____

_____

_____

_____

What happens when salt loses its saltiness? If you were to lose your "saltiness," how effective would your influence on your friends be? _____

_____

_____

_____

_____

_____

_____

💬 Point

If you're like most teenagers, you pride yourself on your loyalty in friendships. Loyalty is a great thing. The problem is, if you have messed-up priorities or a false idea of what loyalty means, you may try to justify your friendships and make excuses for why you can't back out of them, even when your own spiritual health is at stake.

See if you recognize any of these excuses:

1. "If I back out, who is going to reach them? I'm their only Christian friend."

Well, if God was big enough to bring *you* into your friend's life, he is big enough to bring other Christians too. Besides, Jesus never dropped his standards to please others—even though he was the only savior for the whole world. Jesus refused to compromise in order to reach anyone. Neither should you compromise to win an unbelieving friend.

2. "But they won't understand. They'll think I'm a snob!"

Your unbelieving peers may think you're a snob for backing away, but they will be wrong. On the other hand, if you keep compromising in order to hang out with lost friends, those friends will think you are a hypocrite—and this time they will be right.

3. "But my friend is so close to accepting Jesus!"

God knows how close your lost friend is to him. He knows much better than you do. And he is fully capable of doing exactly what is necessary to continue the process. You, meanwhile, need to do what is best for your own spiritual welfare. Consider this: When Jesus fed those twelve thousand people, that was as close as some of them ever got to faith in him—and he still walked away.

4. "But he (or she) is my best friend!"

Well, then, what's best for that friend? Certainly not for you to compromise, grow spiritually weak, and fail to be a positive influence.

The truth is, as a Christian you have not been called to make friends; you have been called to make disciples. Now before you get cynical about that statement, please understand: You can be friends with people and disciple

THE PRIORITIES PRINCIPLE

them at the same time. In fact, the whole thrust of this journal is that discipling friends is a must!

God is not antifriendship. After all, he's the inspiration for the classic "Friends Are Friends Forever"! But your eternal purpose can never take priority over a temporary relationship—not even a "best" relationship. When you are no longer following Christ, you can't lead others—not even your best friend—to him.

Think of the name of the lost friend you feel closest to. Do you care more about that friend or the friendship? Journal your thoughts.

PART TWO:
THE PRINCIPLES

Day THREE

💬 Text

Read 1 Corinthians 10:13.

💬 Test

Are any of the temptations you experience unique to you? _____

_____

_____

_____

Where is the focus of this verse: the temptation or the way out? What should you look for when you find yourself being tempted? _____

_____

_____

_____

_____

_____

_____

💬 Point

How do you know when it's time to back off or bail out of a relationship with an unbelieving friend? In an airline emergency, the timing is obvious. The oxygen masks drop out of the overhead compartment. In a relationship emergency, there are obvious cues as well. For example:

1. When Your Motivation Changes

When it comes to your relationships with lost friends, you must continuously ask, "What's my motivation? Why am I in this relationship?" When a relationship that started out as evangelistic in purpose begins to be more about

THE PRIORITIES PRINCIPLE

having someone to hang out with (or maybe, in the case of the opposite sex, about romance), then it's time to back off or bail out.

2. When the Temptation to Compromise Becomes a Real Battle

There is a difference between being offered something and being tempted with something. Let's say two Christian students are offered a beer. One student is not tempted to drink at all, while the other student finds the temptation almost irresistible. The important thing is to know yourself and know what tempts you. Then you can stay away from those people and environments where temptation is likely to run high.

3. When You Violate One of Your Standards a Second Time

When you find that you've violated a standard twice, you need to back off or bail out of the relationship that's involved. Why twice? Because the first time you violate a standard, you need to go to that friend and apologize for compromising. Your friend will take notice, and chances are you will never violate that standard again.

Besides, as we've said before, failure is sometimes the greatest teacher. But two strikes, and that's it. Don't risk striking out—step away from the batter's box first!

PART TWO:
THE PRINCIPLES

4. When Your Parents Say, "It's Over!"

Maximum freedom is always found under God's authority. That means you need to submit to the authorities that God has placed over you—and Mom and Dad are at the top of the list. Disobedience to your parents is ultimately disobedience to God. Besides, parents (moms especially) have a unique and uncanny insight when it comes to teenagers and their friends. If your parents say no to a relationship with a particular friend, you need to respect their insight and authority.

5. When the Holy Spirit Says, "Back Out"

The Holy Spirit can and will speak to you—but his wisdom and counsel will do you no good if you can't hear him. Only by spending quality time alone with God will you have ears to hear the Spirit's still, small voice. When you sense the Spirit prompting you to back out of a relationship with an unbelieving friend, then back out. When you feel a certain inner hesitancy about a relationship, you must be mature enough to recognize the source of that hesitancy, admit that it exists, and back off. The Holy Spirit can discern all things. He knows what's best for you—and he knows what's best for your friend.

Do you see any of these cues in your relationships with lost friends? What is the Holy Spirit telling you to do? Journal your thoughts here.

THE PRIORITIES PRINCIPLE

Day FOUR

💬 Text

Read Romans 12:3.

💬 Test

How does Paul say you are you to think of yourself? _____

_____

_____

_____

_____

What do you think it means to consider yourself with "sober judgment"?

_____

_____

_____

How can you do this "in accordance with the measure of faith God has given you"? _____

_____

_____

_____

_____

**PART TWO:
THE PRINCIPLES**

💬 Point

The time will come when you realize you need to back off or bail out of a particular relationship. But how will you do it? In the long-term process of influencing a lost teenager for Christ, how you exit a relationship is as important as how you enter it.

Here are two things you must not do:

1. Don't judge.

It's easy to be judgmental toward your lost friends. But pointing a white-gloved finger is no way to exit a relationship.

For one thing, judging an unbelieving friend is literally taking a position that Jesus did not take. Remember the story of Jesus and the woman caught in adultery? Jesus didn't pass judgment; instead, he invited anyone who was without sin to cast the first stone. Backing off or bailing out of a friendship is not an act of judgment; it's an act of wisdom—one that probably has less to do with your friend's problems than with your own weaknesses.

Bailing out of a friendship is not an act of judgment; it's an act of wisdom.

Judging an unbelieving friend is not only wrong, it's counterproductive. Backing off or bailing out is actually part of the process of influence. When you back off, you aren't withdrawing influence; you are setting up and preparing for someone else to continue God's pursuit of your friend. If you exit the relationship with a judgmental attitude, you erect barriers that will only complicate things for the next believer who comes into your friend's life.

2. Don't hide.

This scenario happens too often: A Christian student has invested in an unbelieving friend for an extended period of time. Then he or she recognizes one of the five cues and decides to back off or bail out. What happens? Without any explanation the Christian student disappears. He or she stops returning phone calls and hides from the unbelieving friend at school. This kind of

THE PRIORITIES PRINCIPLE

"disappearing act" completely distorts the love of God that the student had previously worked so hard to exhibit. The lost friend can't help but feel judged and think, *What's wrong with me?*

Don't make excuses! When you back off or bail out of a friendship for the sake of your own spiritual health, be truthful—or risk losing all the ground you gained for Christ in your friend's life.

How can you back off or bail out of a relationship without appearing to be judgmental? Write your thoughts here.

💬 Text

Read Colossians 4:6 and Ephesians 4:15.

💬 Test

What do you think it means to have your conversation "full of grace" and "seasoned with salt"? _____

_____

_____

_____

_____

_____

What do you think it means to speak the truth "in love"? _____

_____

_____

_____

_____

💬 Point

We have created a memorable statement to help you back off or bail out the right way:

Say what is true . . . pray before you do . . . and follow through.

Let's look at each of the components of this statement separately:

1. Say what is true.

You need to tell your unbelieving friend exactly why you are backing off or bailing out. You don't have to go into a long discourse. It can be something as

THE PRIORITIES PRINCIPLE

simple as this: "The most important relationship in my life is the one I have with Jesus Christ. Because I don't want to jeopardize that relationship, our relationship isn't the wisest thing for me to be involved in right now. I need to make God my priority so he can do what he wants to do in me." Honesty is not the best policy; it's the *only* policy.

There is a wrong way to tell the truth, though. Paul says in Colossians 4:6 that our conversation should be "full of grace, seasoned with salt." In other words, we must have grace as our motivation, mindset, and heart. Think of Jesus; he personified grace when he took our sin upon himself so that we might be made right with God. His concern was for us, not for himself. Conversing in grace, then, means that as you speak, you think of your friend first. You say what's best for your friend, not what's "face saving" for you. You don't take the truth and beat your friend over the head with it.

> **There is a wrong way to tell the truth.**

2. Pray before you do.

It's imperative that you seek God and his wisdom before getting into a conversation with a friend about backing off. Many times, through prayer, God will give you special insight into your friend's situation. Other times he will give you sensitivity to the right timing. Still other times God will work out the circumstances so that you barely have to open your mouth. He may move in such a way that your friend is the one who backs off.

3. Make sure you follow through.

If I told you that I believed that for the sake of the health and welfare of my family, I needed to stop traveling and speaking; yet I continued to travel and speak, what would you think of my belief system? You'd laugh in my face if I said, "My family is my top priority." The same principle holds true if you claim, "God is my priority, and I need to back off this relationship," but you don't follow through. You lose credibility—and influence—with your friends.

The truth is, if you're not willing to back off or bail out of friendships that hurt you spiritually, then you're not ready to have relationships with unbelieving friends.

What do you think of that statement? Journal your thoughts.

EXP When Katie told us that she was pledging a sorority at Louisiana State University (one of the top-rated party schools in America), we can honestly say we didn't worry about her. It was not that Katie was perfect. It was not that she was incapable of failing. It was that Katie had an inner strength welded by God that is found in few teenagers. She rushed, joined a sorority, and began to have the kind of influence we pray for all of our students to have. Her standards were definitely tested, but they were proved strong. Over her freshman and sophomore years, she personally invested herself in the lives of her sorority sisters and became the most influential girl in her sorority. Her sorority sisters awarded her the highest award any member can receive.

Imagine our surprise, then, when she told us at the beginning of her junior year that she had decided to quit her sorority. Such a thing is almost unheard of in the collegiate Greek system. You don't quit your sorority—especially in your third year! When we asked her why she was quitting, Katie's answer was simple: "God told me to." She'd heard the Holy Spirit whisper to her. His voice was small and still but obvious: "Quit." So she did.

You might assume that Katie's decision caused her to lose all the influence she had worked so hard to develop with her sorority sisters. Her time there had been wasted. Two years and nothing to show for it. Right? On the contrary, Katie actually gained leverage. Her friends didn't see her as being judgmental. They respected her decision. In fact, her decision only reinforced what she had claimed all along: She belonged to God, and her relationship with him was more important than any other.

She still talks with the girls. Many come to her and ask her for advice about life. She has been a bridesmaid in several sorority sisters' weddings. And when Katie got married, many of her sorority sisters were in attendance.

PART TWO:
THE PRINCIPLES

It seems clear that God wanted Katie to bail out, not because her friendships were putting her in spiritual danger, but in order to increase her leverage—to actually maximize her influence with her sorority sisters. She listened to his still, small voice, and both she and her friends were blessed as a result.

To become a student of influence like Katie, you need to be in such intimate communion with God that you, too, can hear the Holy Spirit's whisper. He may whisper, "Back off," because a particular friendship is putting your relationship with Christ in jeopardy. Or he may whisper, "Bail out," because he has someone else he wants to bring into your friend's life to lead the next leg of the journey.

This weekend think about the relationships you have with your lost friends. Pray for each one. Ask the Holy Spirit to give you wisdom to know how to proceed for the sake of your spiritual health, God's kingdom, and your friend's journey toward faith in Christ.

THE PRIORITIES PRINCIPLE

Principle

You must maintain effective accountability relationships with other Christian students.

Critical Question

Are you accountable to other Christians?

Key Passage

Galatians 6:1–2

PRINCIPLE 3

The Accountability Principle
Making Sure Someone Has Your Back

**My best friend is the one
who brings out the best in me.**

HENRY FORD

The Accountability Principle
Making Sure Someone Has Your Back

A couple of years ago, *CCM* magazine ran an awesome interview with the members of the rock group P.O.D. As you know, this foursome from San Diego, California, has taken the rock-and-roll and MTV world by storm, garnering nominations for both Grammy and MTV video awards. They've also been extremely vocal, both personally and musically, about their relationship with Jesus Christ. Asked about the band's perspective on faith and their calling to reach people with the gospel, Sonny, the lead singer, said this:

> I believe there is a forefront, and on this side is the kingdom of heaven, and on that side is the lost, dying world. P.O.D. has always been folded over on this fence. There are people right up front with us, embracing us, holding onto our legs, strapping us down. On the other side, our hands are going as far as they can, trying to pull the lost into the kingdom of heaven. When you're standing way back on the outskirts, of course you are going to have concerns, because you are looking from a distance. You're wondering, "What's going on over there? Half-way in, half-way out!" But praise God! God has surrounded us with what we need. Kids come out, and they are like, "Dude, I get it."[1]

Did you see it? The visual imagery is powerful: To be an influence without being influenced, you need fellow believers in your life who will hold on to your ankles as you reach out over the fence to your lost peers. That's a picture of accountability. Clearly God wants you to lean into the dark and pull your friends to safety. But without effective accountability, the likelihood that you will fall over the fence is pretty high. You must have someone—or many someones—who will strap you down. You must have accountability relationships with mature Christian friends who will ask you the hard questions. Friends who will not let you drift away. Friends who will make sure you keep your relationship with Christ the priority.

This is not an option—it's a must! Do you want to be a student of influence? Then the principle of accountability must be nonnegotiable.

Day
ONE

PART TWO:
THE PRINCIPLES

Text

Read Exodus 17:8–16.

Test

What role did Aaron and Hur play in Moses' life? _____

_____

_____

_____

_____

What happened as long as Moses' hands were lifted? _____

_____

_____

_____

_____

_____

Point

Accountability has been a Christian buzzword for some time. But, like many things in postmodern Christianity, the word has gradually become diluted and misused to such a degree that few students today really understand its meaning or purpose.

In our experience, student accountability groups tend to quickly degenerate into glorified "Sinners Anonymous" meetings that go something like this: "Hi, my name is Larry, and I struggle with lust." Everyone replies, "Hi, Larry! We lust too." Then they all pray, "God, help us not to struggle with lust," and move on. Or, "Hi, my name is Sarah, and my issue is jealousy." Everyone replies, "Hi, Sarah! We struggle with jealousy too." Then they pray, "God, help us not to struggle with jealousy," and move on. Or the group leader reads a list of potential sins, and, as each sin is named, those who are guilty for that week raise their hands. Then it's on to the next sin. No one takes responsibility for anyone else; they just admit they're all in the same boat.

That is *not* functional accountability! But what is? Here's our definition:

Accountability means giving an individual or group permission to question you in one or more aspects of your life and committing yourself to total honesty with that individual or group.

Permission is a key word. Accountability is a two-way street. If you try to hold someone accountable in areas which you have not been given permission to ask questions, you won't succeed—and vice versa.

Nor will you succeed if you only talk in generalities. You need to get specific about the aspects of life where you desire accountability. What specific area of temptation do you struggle with? Late-night movies? Certain types of music by certain artists? Thoughts about a certain person of the opposite sex? Perhaps you need accountability in the area of spending consistent time alone with God or in the area of submission to authority. You know (in theory at least) that maximum freedom is found under God's authority; yet rebellion against Mom and Dad is a frequent struggle. Or perhaps you need accountability in a particular "trouble spot" in a relationship with an unbelieving friend. Whatever the case, the more specific you are about your need, the better you can be held accountable to a godly standard.

In an effective accountability relationship, you should be able to share anything—your biggest temptations, your deepest hurts, your greatest frustrations. To do so, however, requires a commitment on your part to total honesty. You have to be real about who you are and what you're going

THE ACCOUNTABILITY PRINCIPLE

through. An accountability relationship built on lies eventually dies. Accountability and dishonesty simply cannot coexist.

When your own battle rages, do you have someone you can depend on to "hold up your hands," as Aaron and Hur did for Moses? Who are you accountable to? Record your thoughts here.

_____

_____

_____

_____

_____

_____

_____

_____

_____

_____

_____

_____

_____

_____

_____

_____

_____

_____

_____

**PART TWO:
THE PRINCIPLES**

Day
TWO

🗨 Text

Read Luke 17:3–5.

🗨 Test

According to Jesus, how should we approach other Christians who have fallen into sin? _____

_____

_____

_____

_____

_____

Why do you think the disciples responded, "Increase our faith"? _____

_____

_____

_____

_____

_____

🗨 Point

Whenever we teach on accountability, we have students who come up and tell us, "I don't need to have someone in my life to hold me accountable. My relationship with God is between me and God—and no one else."

Nothing could be further from the truth. Yes, a relationship with God is personal. But it's not intended to be private. There's a big difference. Let's say it a little louder:

A relationship with God is personal . . . but it's not private.

The confusion some teenagers have about this subject is understandable. After all, Christianity is distinguished from other religions in that it is personal. Through Christ you have a personal relationship with the Creator of the universe. The Spirit of God resides personally in your heart. No other belief system makes even remotely similar claims.

> **Intimacy with God does not relieve you from accountability to the body of Christ.**

But at no point does the intimacy of your walk with God relieve you from personal accountability to the body of Christ. Your relationship with God is not just your business, and my relationship with God is not just mine. We are accountable to one another. Why do we say that? Because Jesus himself commands us to practice accountability! He considered accountability so important that he commanded his disciples to hold one another accountable. That's what Luke 17:3–4 is all about.

You probably don't like the idea of being confronted about your sins or weaknesses by other Christians. You're in good company. Neither did the disciples. How do we know? Look at their response: "Increase our faith!" (Luke 17:5).

You get the sense from this verse that the disciples looked wide-eyed at Jesus and said, "Dude, I can't do that! You are going to have to amp up the faith quotient in me, because I am not about to take instruction or get rebuked by these guys. I'll take it from you, Jesus—but these bozos? No way!"

But Jesus was making a point to his disciples and to us: We are in one another's lives for this very purpose. Accountability is my responsibility. It's your responsibility too.

PART TWO:
THE PRINCIPLES

Journal your thoughts about this statement: "Your relationship with God is personal . . . but it is not private."

THE ACCOUNTABILITY PRINCIPLE

Day
THREE

💬 Text

Read 1 Corinthians 12:12–27.

💬 Test

Based on these verses, how would you describe the way the body of Christ is intended to function? _____

_____

_____

_____

_____

_____

In what ways are the different parts of the body accountable to one another? How does accountability benefit each part? _____

_____

_____

_____

_____

_____

_____

_____

**PART TWO:
THE PRINCIPLES**

💬 Point

The concept of the connectivity of the body of Christ may seem strange to you. But Scripture plainly tells us that we are all individual parts of one body. In 1 Corinthians 12:12, Paul says that we are all one unit, even though we're made up of many parts. That means you can't say, "Well, I don't really want to be accountable to those people, so I won't be a part of that unit." When you become a believer, you become a part of the body of Christ. End of story. And that throws your lot in with other Christians forever. Which is a good thing. You need the other parts of the body in order to function and grow.

If you're an eye without an ear, how can you hear? If you're an ear without a nose, how can you smell?

What would happen to your hand if it decided it did not need any input or help from the rest of the body? Without the arm, the hand can't function. Without the brain, the hand can't function. Without the heart, the hand can't function. The implication is clear. Without the rest of the body, that hand, at the very least, would never fulfill its purpose; at worst, it would be rendered useless.

The same principle applies to you. You need the rest of the body of Christ in order to find and fulfill your God-given purpose. That's the way God designed it. Christians need other Christians.

Think about what happens when you stub your big toe on the bedpost in the middle of the night. Nerves in your big toe send a signal to your brain, reporting pain in the South Pole region. Your brain immediately sends out an all-points bulletin. Your eyes respond by tearing up. Your mouth and vocal chords respond by screaming (we won't try to guess *what*). Your hand responds by grabbing your toe. Your good leg responds by jumping up and down. And all these things happen in a matter of split seconds! All the parts of your body respond to the need of that one part.

> **Christians need other Christians.**

THE ACCOUNTABILITY PRINCIPLE

If you refuse to establish strong accountability relationships, you are like a big toe that has no one to care for it when it's injured. You are like a hand that decides it doesn't need input or help from the rest of the body. You risk having a life of loneliness, pain, spiritual impotence—and zero influence with your peers.

How could greater accountability help you at this point in your journey to become a student of influence? Journal your thoughts.

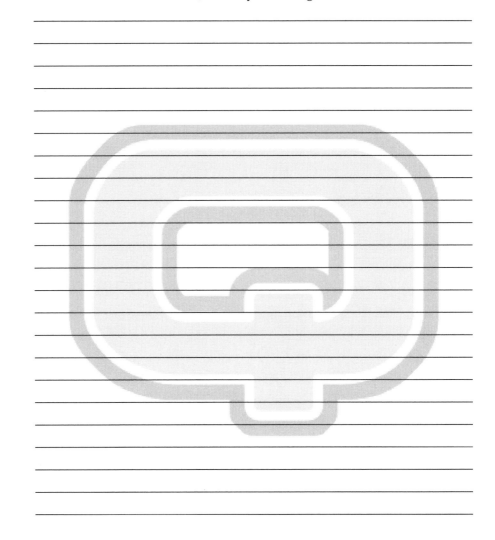

_____

_____

_____

_____

_____

_____

_____

_____

_____

_____

_____

_____

_____

_____

_____

_____

_____

_____

_____

_____

_____

_____

PART TWO:
THE PRINCIPLES

Day
FOUR

🗨 Text

Read Ephesians 6:13–17.

🗨 Test

What areas of the body does the armor of God cover? Why do these areas need to be protected spiritually? _____

_____

_____

_____

_____

_____

_____

What one area is not covered by the armor of God? _____

_____

_____

_____

🗨 Point

We all need accountability to encourage us to do our best. It is a fact of life: Most of us do better when we know someone is checking up on us. In almost every facet of life, what is *expected* is connected to what is *inspected*. Would you study as hard in school if there were no tests? (Maybe that's not a good illustration.) Would athletes practice as hard if the coach just handed them the ball and sent them out to practice without him?

We need accountability for another reason too. We all have weaknesses—"chinks in our armor," so to speak. We try to cover them up, but eventually they get found out. You can count on it: Your weaknesses will manifest

THE ACCOUNTABILITY PRINCIPLE

themselves sooner or later. Either someone who cares about you will point out your shortcomings to you, or your shortcomings will wind up being exposed in public. The only question is, how do you want a particular weakness to be exposed?

If you are going to be influential, you must have strong accountability relationships with friends who care enough about you to speak up about your weaknesses before someone else does. Hearing something negative from a friend is tough, but the alternative—hearing it from someone else, perhaps in an embarrassing public moment—is a whole lot more painful. Sometimes we like to tell one another, "I've got your back." The truth is, you need friends who will do exactly that.

> **Accountability can save you from hurt and negative consequences.**

Think of Paul's challenge in Ephesians 6 to put on the full armor of God. He says you need to put on the belt of truth, the breastplate of righteousness, the shield of faith, and the helmet of salvation; to fit your feet with readiness; and to pick up the sword of the Spirit. (If you were in one of our classes on this subject, you might see a student dressed in a weight belt, a catcher's chest protector, a garbage can lid, a football helmet, combat boots, and a toy sword.)

In practical terms, these pieces of armor defend your midsection, torso, feet, and head—basically the entire front portion of your body. But that leaves one critical area exposed: your back. And that's where most of the enemy's attacks will come from: the back, where you're not looking.

Therein lies the beauty of God's design for accountability. When you enter into accountability relationships with other Christians, you stand back to back with one another. No area is exposed to the enemy. You can see the attacks

coming at each other's backs and head them off. You can cover the chinks in one another's armor.

Who has *your* back? Can you think of an instance in your life when accountability could have saved you from hurt or negative consequences? Journal your thoughts and feelings.

_____

_____

_____

_____

_____

_____

_____

_____

_____

_____

_____

_____

_____

_____

_____

_____

_____

_____

_____

_____

_____

_____

THE ACCOUNTABILITY PRINCIPLE

Day FIVE

Text

Read 2 Chronicles 10:1–19.

Test

Who were the two "accountability groups" in Rehoboam's life? Which group do you think he should have listened to? _____

_____

_____

_____

_____

_____

What was Rehoboam's mistake? What were the consequences? _____

_____

_____

_____

_____

_____

_____

**PART TWO:
THE PRINCIPLES**

Point

Choosing the wrong person to hold you accountable is as dangerous as not being accountable at all—if not more so. It's the equivalent of going off to war with someone, fighting back to back, and then realizing too late that he or she is not as well trained, battle ready, and anxious to live as you are. To match yourself with such a person could prove fatal!

How do you choose the right person for an accountability relationship?

1. Choose someone you can trust.

Trust is the currency of relationship. It's what allows authenticity and vulnerability to emerge. And if these characteristics don't become a part of the fabric of your accountability relationship, then the accountability will be ineffective, at best.

2. Choose someone to hold you accountable—not someone for you to hold accountable.

The question is not "Who can I hold accountable?" It's "Who can hold *me* accountable?" Asking the correct question will cause you to gravitate toward a spiritually strong accountability partner who will hold you to a high standard—as opposed to someone spiritually weaker who will allow you to drop down to his or her level.

3. Choose someone of the same gender.

Nothing is more dangerous or inherently ineffective than accountability between students of the opposite sex. For one thing, authenticity is hard to develop between girls and guys because hormones and attraction disguise themselves as trust. The fact is, the desire for acceptance is at its peak in guy-girl relationships. Real trust can't be built if students are simply "performing" to gain acceptance.

For another thing, guys and girls generally struggle with different issues. Guys in a co-ed accountability group will get frustrated quickly if they have to listen to a young lady talk nonstop about her struggle with self-esteem. Conversely, the girls in a co-ed group will never want to date boys again if they hear how often their brothers in Christ struggle with their thoughts.

Finally, because effective accountability is intended to be a deeply meaningful, spiritual experience, an accountability relationship between a

THE ACCOUNTABILITY PRINCIPLE

girl and a guy can all too easily take a romantic turn. Holding hands to pray becomes holding hands to play, and accountability is out the window.

4. Choose someone based on your particular accountability needs.

Once you pinpoint the area or areas in which you require accountability, you can base your choice of an accountability partner on your particular needs. Obviously you need a partner who has a track record of success in the area in question. A friend who has the same struggles you do won't be much help. You may find that your best choice is someone who is older than you are— possibly an adult. And you may need to be accountable to different people on different issues.

In what areas do you need accountability? Who could you ask to hold you accountable in these areas? Spend some time praying for wisdom and guidance, and journal what the Holy Spirit is speaking to you.

_____

_____

_____

_____

_____

_____

_____

_____

_____

_____

_____

_____

_____

E⟨X⟩P Clearly, accountability is in every Christian student's best interest. So why, with all the positive ramifications of accountability, do some still resist it? In a word: confrontation. Students resist accountability because they hate confrontation.

This is really a problem for all of us—students and adults. We don't like to confront someone because we are more concerned about what that person thinks about us than we are about his or her spiritual life. We don't develop a true accountability relationship because we want to maintain the friendship at all costs. We don't want to build up and strengthen our friend at the risk of having that person be unhappy with us.

Coach Mike Krzyzewski relates a story that illustrates this principle beautifully. Two of his freshman players, Johnny Dawkins and Mark Alerie, were late for a team bus. Coach K remembers: "We didn't know where they were, they had not called, and every other member of the team was on time. So we left them behind. Eventually the two caught up with us, and I remember being ready to hammer them. But after hearing that they had overslept, I began to wonder why other members of our team had not checked up on them."[2] I can tell you why the other teammates didn't check on them: They didn't want to make those guys (Dawkins and Alerie) mad at them for waking them up! They were more concerned about the friendship than they were the friend.

You can't love people without accepting them, but you can accept people without truly loving them. In a friendship where acceptance is the priority, confrontation rarely happens. Neither friend loves the other enough to say the things that really need to be said and possibly risk the friendship.

A true friend is someone who accepts you just as you are, but who loves you too much to leave you that way. Think of the tragic deaths of comedians

THE ACCOUNTABILITY PRINCIPLE

John Candy, Chris Farley, and John Belushi. How many times did we hear people on TV claim, "Oh, he was one of my best friends"? Yet they never confronted their "best friend" on his alcohol, food, or drug abuse. They chose to ignore these obvious danger signals for the sake of being accepted by their famous buddy. Apparently they were more committed to the friendship than the friend.

This weekend, as you spend time with your friends, evaluate each relationship on this basis: Can you speak the truth in love to that friend? Can he or she speak the truth in love to you? Which has the higher priority in your relationship: love or acceptance?

PART TWO:
THE PRINCIPLES

Principle

You must love and accept your unbelieving
peers unconditionally.

Critical Question

Do you unconditionally accept your lost friends?

Key Passage

Romans 15:7

PRINCIPLE 4

The Unconditional-Acceptance Principle
Out-Loving the World

There is the great lesson of
"Beauty and the Beast":
that a thing must be loved
before it is loveable.

G. K. CHESTERTON

The Unconditional-Acceptance Principle
Out-Loving the World

If you're like most teenagers, you don't really choose your friends. You gravitate toward those people who accept you. It's as if you and your peers have built-in acceptance radar. You are drawn toward people and environments of acceptance.

Think about it. You didn't set up a table in the high-school foyer on the first day of your freshman year with a big sign that read Accepting Applications for Friends Here! (If you had, your classmates would have ostracized you for the remainder of your existence.) You don't "try out" friends the way athletes try out for the football or volleyball team. No, who you build relationships with has more to do with who is willing to accept you than who matches up to a predetermined checklist of desirable characteristics.

Acceptance is an incredibly powerful desire in all human beings. It causes men and women, young and old, to abandon their integrity and convictions. For you and your friends in the high-school years, this desire is magnified tenfold. It's so powerful that it transcends and overrides any person or group of people. It trumps integrity, convictions, and the welfare of the very people from whom acceptance is sought. For many of your friends (not you, of course!), acceptance by a friend is more important than the friend. When acceptance is at stake, there's almost nothing they won't do.

The fact is, acceptance and influence are inexorably linked. You can be immovably committed to God. You can have rock-solid standards. You can have great people surrounding you and holding you down in the hurricane of maximum dynamic pressure. But if you don't accept your lost friends unconditionally, all is for naught. You disqualify yourself in the battle for influence. Your friends will resist your influence if they perceive that you don't accept them. If they feel accepted, however, they will drop their guard.

As Christians we have experienced the unconditional acceptance of a heavenly Father who loved us "while we were still sinners" (Romans 5:8). We should be the most accepting people and provide the most accepting environments a lost student could possibly experience. Unfortunately, too many churches fail in this regard. By being more judgmental than accepting, they push unbelievers away.

To be influential you must out-accept the competition. Many teenagers with less-than-desirable lifestyles and belief systems are out there right now, accepting your lost friends. Are you going to stand by and let unbelieving teens out-love and out-accept you?

You know you're becoming a student of influence if your answer is a resounding "No way!"

Day
ONE

💬 Text

Read 1 Corinthians 12:31 and 13:1–8.

💬 Test

What is "the most excellent way"? _____

_____

_____

_____

How do you think love translates into influence?_____

_____

_____

_____

_____

_____

💬 Point

Is there a "best way" to influence others for Christ? According to Scripture, the answer is yes. There *is* a best way to live a life of standards, priorities, and accountability—and a life that will have a positive, powerful influence on others. Paul calls it the "most excellent way" in 1 Corinthians 12:31.

This verse, interestingly enough, follows a discussion on spiritual gifts and the different parts of the body of Christ. You get the sense that the Corinthian Christians were struggling with the idea that everyone has different gifts and brings different strengths (and weaknesses) to the church. Apparently many people were competing to be considered the more "important" parts.

When Paul mentions "the most excellent way" (sounds like Wayne and Garth from *Wayne's World*), he is referring to the right way for believers to exercise spiritual gifts. He does not identify love as a gift. Rather, love is a fruit of the Spirit—and it supercedes the gifts of the Spirit. The implication here is huge. You can't use the gift of prophesy as an excuse to speak and act condescendingly and harshly toward others. The spiritual gift of evangelism does not free you from showing unconditional love.

Love always trumps any gift you may have. It overrides any mission you are seeking to accomplish. Zeal to see your lost friends come to faith in Christ must never take precedence over the love you are to display in the process. Too many Christian students make the mistake of speaking words in scrutiny and judgment—words that are technically true but should have been spoken in love and acceptance. No wonder lost teenagers run!

Do you tend to interact with your peers from a heart of scrutiny and judgment? How can you begin to apply "the most excellent way" to your relationships with your lost friends? Journal your thoughts.

Day
TWO

🗩 Text

Read 1 Corinthians 13:1–2 and Ephesians 4:29.

🗩 Test

Without love as their motivation, what do your words sound like to others? _____

_____

_____

What types of words should and should not come out of your mouth? What do your words have to do with influence? _____

_____

_____

_____

_____

_____

_____

_____

**PART TWO:
THE PRINCIPLES**

🗩 Point

To become influential with your peers, you must learn to leverage your words. That means restraining yourself from speaking words that are unwholesome—literally, words that are "rotten, unfit for use, potentially damaging." The picture Paul paints in Ephesians 4:29 is of a screen over your mouth or a restraining leash on your tongue. Just as a pit bull will attack if his leash is removed, so your tongue, which is by nature a "restless evil" (James 3:8), will do damage if you allow it to.

By using restraint, however, you can leverage your words for good in the lives of your lost friends. The question you must continually ask yourself is, "Will the words I'm about to speak build my friend up or tear my friend down?" The issue is motivation. Unconditional acceptance calls for speaking from a heart that is more interested in helping than hurting, more interested in loving than judging.

In fact, Paul says in Ephesians 4:15 that you should "speak the truth in love." The implication is that truth can be told in a way that will either help others or hurt others. There are no neutral words. Listeners deposit every word spoken to them in one of two banks: hurtful or helpful.

When you speak the truth in love—when you speak from a motivation of building others up rather than tearing them down—you accumulate spiritual collateral in your friends' lives. And eventually you will find that you can draw upon this collateral as leverage for influence. Without love behind your words, however, everything you say is worthless. You're nothing more than "a resounding gong or a clanging cymbal," as Paul says in 1 Corinthians 13:1.

There is an old adage that goes, "People don't care what you know until they know that you care." You discount and discredit all that you know about God and his love when you don't exemplify that love in your words and in your life. You cause a disconnect of monumental proportions in the hearts and minds of your lost friends. In effect, you unplug your potential for influence.

What impact are you having on your lost friends' lives based on the words you speak to them? Would you say that you are most effective at building up or tearing down? Write your thoughts here.

_____

_____

_____

_____

_____

THE UNCONDITIONAL-ACCEPTANCE PRINCIPLE

Day THREE

💬 Text

Read 1 Corinthians 13:4–8.

💬 Test

What are the characteristics of true, biblical love?_____

_____

_____

Which of these characteristics come easiest to you? Which ones do you struggle with the most? _____

_____

_____

_____

💬 Point

Perhaps you feel that you just can't do it. You can't love unconditionally. It's unnatural. It's too much of a struggle. You don't feel like accepting your lost peers. But there is a major flaw in that line of thinking.

Stuart's dad had a massive heart attack several years ago. He survived, but since then he has faced the toughest task of his life: coping mentally with his mortality after his near-brush with death. Doctors have said that the best thing he can do for his heart is to exercise. But if you're a victim of a heart attack, that recommendation seems counterintuitive. You live with the ever-constant realization that your heart is weak. And you have the ever-constant fear that physical exertion will bring on another attack. That's why many heart patients don't follow their doctor's orders to get the exercise they need.

You don't exercise your heart because it *is* in shape; you exercise your heart *to get it* in shape.

Like physical exercise, spiritual exercise is an act of the will—a feeling-defying act of the will. You force yourself to exercise. You force yourself to love. It's a choice.

You may object, "Well, I'm just not a very accepting person." But that's no excuse to reject the unlovable.

You may say, "I just don't love easily." But that's no excuse to be judgmental and harsh.

You may say, "I have a hard time giving." But that's no excuse to be selfish with your time, energy, and heart.

The assumption behind such statements is this: "If my heart ever changes, then I will start unconditionally loving and accepting my lost friend." That's like saying, "Well, if I ever wake up with the energy to exercise, I'll start exercising. If I wake up with a smaller appetite, I'll eat less. If I wake up and find I've lost my taste for ice cream, I'll cut back on Dairy Queen."

Unconditional love doesn't come naturally to our selfish hearts. We don't wake up one morning and have it. We have to make the choice and just do it. Contrary to everything you might hear on *As the World Turns*, you don't *fall* in love; you *choose* to love, and then you do what it takes to start loving.

Jesus didn't fall to earth, say, "Uh-oh," and decide that he would die on the cross for humanity. Jesus didn't *fall* in love with humanity. From the beginning of time, he *chose* to love mankind and to die for our sins and for his Father's glory. His love was a choice. Your love is a choice too.

How hard is it for you to love your lost peers unconditionally? What keeps you from making the choice to love and then follow through? Journal your thoughts.

_____

_____

_____

THE UNCONDITIONAL–ACCEPTANCE PRINCIPLE

PART TWO:
THE PRINCIPLES

Day FOUR

Text

Read Matthew 5:43–48.

Test

What was the common wisdom of Jesus' day regarding who you should love? What did he teach that was radically different? _____

_____

_____

_____

_____

_____

Why should you love people who give you a hard time? _____

_____

_____

_____

_____

Point

To love people who don't share your beliefs or live by your standards is a difficult decision to make—and an even harder one to carry out. But here's the bottom line:

You can't express or experience unconditional love unless you are with people and in environments that are inconsistent and different from you.

Your lost friends *will* be different. Their lives *will* be inconsistent with your

Christian values and beliefs. That's what makes the choice to love and accept them unconditionally so difficult—and so necessary.

Unfortunately, many students fail to make the choice to love. They have an "an eye for an eye and a tooth for a tooth" mentality:

- If you reject me, then I'll reject you.

- If you don't come to my church, then I'm not going to come to your deal.

- If you don't return my calls, I'm going to stop trying to reach you.

- If you don't express interest in my stuff, then I won't express interest in your stuff.

How easy it is to devolve into this kind of thinking! The problem is, when you go this route, you end up treating your lost friends the way those friends treat you—or worse.

When Jesus came into the world, the "eye for an eye" kind of thinking was the normal way for people to respond in relationships. It was even taught by many of the teachers of that day: If someone mistreats you, you mistreat that person back. If someone is good to you, you be good to that person in return. You may forgive someone three times, but no one can expect you to forgive four, five, or six times. Love the people who love you and hate the people you consider your enemies.

That was the relational standard of the culture until Jesus showed up and changed everything with his teaching in Matthew 5:43–48. According to Jesus, we are not as different from unbelievers as we think we are. The sun rises on the lost and the found. Rain falls on the Christian student and the unbelieving student. We all have been created in the image of God.

PART TWO:
THE PRINCIPLES

Showing unconditional acceptance only to those people whose lives are consistent with our own is no credit to us. If the only people we accept are the people who accept us, then we are not really very accepting, are we? Pagans do that much!

The truth is, most of us are more concerned with living comfortably than loving and accepting our friends unconditionally. In order to be a student of influence, however, you have to answer this question in the affirmative: "Are you willing to express unconditional love to those people within your sphere of influence who are different from you and whose lives are inconsistent with yours?"

What is your response? Journal it here.

Day
FIVE

💬 Text

Read 2 Corinthians 5:18–21.

💬 Test

What is the message of reconciliation? What is the ministry of reconciliation? _____

_____

_____

_____

_____

_____

What does it mean to you to be Christ's ambassador? _____

_____

_____

_____

_____

_____

PART TWO:
THE PRINCIPLES

💬 Point

Reconciliation means "making two conflicting things compatible." And that's your job: to make your lost friends, who are in conflict with God because of their sin, compatible with God. Your unconditional acceptance is the relational bridge that connects one side to the other and allows reconciliation to occur.

Do you remember the day you became a Christian? Something incredible happened. But you didn't do anything to make it happen; only God did. He single-handedly cleared away everything that blocked the way for you to be in relationship with him. He didn't wait for you to deal with your sin on your own. (If he had, he would still be waiting.) No, God did it all. He changed you to make you compatible to himself.

Why, then, do so many Christian students think they have to wait for their peers to change before they can offer their friendship? They do the opposite of what the ministry of rec-onciliation calls them to do. Their message to their friends goes like this: "I've got great news! You can be reconciled to God. You just can't be reconciled to me. God has forgiven you of all your sins, and he wants a relationship with you. But I haven't forgiven you for your differences and your inconsistencies, and you can't have a relationship with me. You see, I have a higher standard than God."

> **Reconciliation is about compatibility, not conformity.**

When you take this approach, you are refusing to do for your friends what God in Christ has done for you. And you reveal to the world that you really don't understand and appreciate your own salvation.

The goal of reconciliation is to develop a relationship built upon acceptance—despite a friend's past. Despite a friend's lifestyle. Despite a friend's flawed ideas about or disagreements with God. Reconciliation is about compatibility, not conformity. Making two conflicting things compatible does not require making them conform first. To think otherwise is like thinking you have to get in the shower and clean up before you can get in the shower and clean up.

Here's a simple formula for you to remember:

THE UNCONDITIONAL–ACCEPTANCE PRINCIPLE

Reconciliation + Relationship = Influence

Your willingness to love and accept your friends unconditionally is the one thing that paves the way to reconciliation, relationship, and ultimately influence for the sake of Christ. Yes, reconciliation can be messy. Reconciliation takes time. It can be all-consuming. But it—not judgment—must be the goal. You have been given a ministry as an ambassador for Christ. God is making his appeal through you. And that means, as a friend of ours, David Crowder, likes to say, his love needs to be "big and loud" in your life.

When it comes to reconciliation, do you have a higher standard than God? Journal your thoughts.

_____

_____

_____

_____

_____

_____

_____

_____

_____

_____

_____

_____

_____

_____

_____

_____

PART TWO:
THE PRINCIPLES

EXP Put down this book right now, hightail it to your nearest pet store, purchase a turtle, and bring it home. Now hand the turtle over to your little brother or sister or a small group of neighborhood kids. Watch to see if the turtle will stick its head out.

My own children thought they had gotten a defective turtle when they found one in the woods behind our home. Why? The turtle would never stick its head out of its shell. But who could blame the turtle? It was being poked with sticks, pencils, and whatever else the kids could find in an attempt to make it reveal its face. Who wouldn't hide?

We can learn a lesson from turtles. When a turtle doesn't feel safe, it retreats to the comfort and protection of its shell. The only time it will stick its head out is when it perceives that the environment is safe enough to do so. A wise turtle owner will get a box, fill it with grass, add a small bowl of water, and wait. Over time the turtle will learn to trust the safety of the environment, and it will reveal its head.

Poking and prodding a lost friend—just like poking and prodding a turtle—is counterproductive. The more you press unbelieving peers about faith issues, the deeper they will retreat into their shells. The better approach is to do everything you can to make your relationship with your friend a safe haven. Only in an environment of acceptance will he or she be willing to open up and seriously consider the message of reconciliation you have to share.

Reconciliation is a messy business, to be sure. Acceptance means dirt and all. It's very possible that you will have to shoulder the weight of consequences and complications that result from your friend's sin. You may have to clean up some messes. You will certainly have to deal with the ramifications of your friend's irresponsibility and inconsistency. Add to these things the fact

THE UNCONDITIONAL-ACCEPTANCE PRINCIPLE

that other Christians will probably make fun of you for being in relationship with someone who screws up. And then consider that your friend may never acknowledge your deep sacrifice and unconditional love.

Reconciliation is definitely a straight shot to Max Q.

Yet, in the process, you are paving the way to influence. And you are following the example of Jesus. Paul puts it this way: "God made him who had no sin to be sin for us, so that in him we might become the righteousness of God" (2 Corinthians 5:21). Jesus became sin for you. He took the burden of your sin and the consequences of your sin and shouldered the weight so that you can have a relationship with God. Now he calls you to do the same for your friend.

This weekend think about the ramifications of this statement for your life:

Acceptance and love are the way of Christ.
They are also the way of a student of influence.

PART TWO:
THE PRINCIPLES

page
168

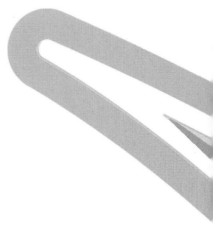

Principle

You must sustain the influence you gain with
your unbelieving peers.

Critical Question

Are you sustaining your influence with your lost friends?

Key Passage

Matthew 5:14–16

PRINCIPLE 5

The Sustained-Influence Principle
Sustaining the Influence You've Gained

I think the dilemma is whether the believing students,
the followers of Jesus, are going to cloister together and keep
singing worship songs over and over and enjoy their faith and
their walk with Christ 'til the end—or whether they're going to let
God's heart start beating inside of their heart. If that happens,
it's going to break their heart and propel them outside of their
circles and outside of their buildings.

LOUIE GIGLIO

The Sustained-Influence Principle
Sustaining the Influence You've Gained

It's no secret that we live in a culture of immediate gratification and instantly met needs. These days you can, in a matter of minutes, drive through and order your lunch, pick up your dry cleaning, withdraw your money, and wash your car. You can drive through just about anything. There are even drive-through mortuaries to make viewing a deceased loved one quicker and easier.

Then, of course, we have the miracle of modern surgery to make people thinner and more attractive overnight. My wife and I watched in amazement as a single guy on a reality TV show got calf implants to make his calf muscles bigger. Apparently he was in pursuit of an instant, perfect calf muscle. Working out was taking too long, so he decided to have implant surgery to obtain his objective *now*.

People will go to hefty extremes for the sake of immediate satisfaction and comfort! And none of us is immune to this dynamic. We may not be the plastic-surgery types, but each of us has developed a certain level of impatience. If something begins to take longer than we expected it to, we can easily lose focus and motivation. It's as if we have a built-in clock inside us that sounds an alarm when things start to draw out too long. If that clock ever strikes midnight, we don't hesitate to move on to something or someone else.

This type of mindset is pervasive in our society. It's especially evident in the student culture. And it's an enemy of influence, which requires a commitment to consistency over time.

A hypothesis in the relatively unknown field of "chaos theory" says that a butterfly fluttering its wings in one part of the world can set in motion a chain of events that will lead to a hurricane in another part of the world. (Which makes you wonder: Just how big is this butterfly? Are we talking a pterodactyl-like, Jurassic Park-sized butterfly? How come we don't hear about this butterfly on the Weather Channel? It sure would give a whole new meaning to the song "Butterfly Kisses.")

It's hard to believe that the simple, repetitive movement of a butterfly's wings could end up causing hurricane-force winds. But seemingly impossible things like this are proven true all the time. For example, science has shown that a piece of cork exerting consistent force over time against a wrecking ball hanging from a crane will eventually move the wrecking ball. If enough time is allowed, the cork will eventually move the wrecking ball with enough force to actually destroy something.

This picture of consistency over time is a perfect illustration of the sustained influence you need to develop. You are the butterfly. You are the cork. Your standards, priorities, accountability, and unconditional acceptance lived out consistently over time create the staging ground for sustained influence with your lost friends.

Are you ready to flap your wings?

Day
ONE

Text

Read Luke 15:1–10.

Test

What characteristics do these two stories have in common? _____

_____

_____

_____

_____

What is the point Jesus was trying to make? _____

_____

_____

_____

Point

For many Christian teenagers, the desire for immediate gratification carries over into the realm of influencing their friends for Christ. They want their friends to receive the free gift of salvation *now*. And if *now* is *later*, then they move on. After all, aren't there too many other teenagers out there who don't know about God, who need his love, and who may be more likely to bend to their methods of persuasion?

Don't get us wrong. You *should* have a passion to see your friends come to Christ as soon as possible. But the idea of immediate accomplishment as it relates to evangelism does not sit well with the example set for us by Jesus in the Gospels. Jesus was never in a hurry. He never operated as if he were under a time crunch.

Consider the two parables he told in Luke 15:1–10 about a shepherd looking for a lost sheep and a woman searching for a lost coin. Notice the shepherd didn't say, "Well, I have ninety-nine other sheep that need my attention and care. Losing one is no big deal." The woman didn't say, "Well, I have nine other coins. Losing one is no big deal." No, both the shepherd and the woman searched frantically until they found what they were looking for. They left the found to search for the lost. And they didn't find what they were looking for immediately. The unspoken implication here is that it took time for the sheep and the coin to be found. The shepherd and the woman were willing to invest whatever amount of time it took to find what was lost.

To be a student of influence among your peers, you must develop patience and reject the mindset that says, "If at first you don't succeed, find someone else." Your influence must not be so superficial that it fades like a summer tan. Rather, your goal must be to consistently influence your friends over time—however long it takes.

Most of your peers will not immediately give their lives to Christ. In fact, for the majority of them, the process will be long and difficult. Months or even years of sustained influence may be necessary in order for God to unravel their past, address their present, and satisfy their questions to the point that his beauty becomes too overwhelming for them to resist.

Influence sustained over time breeds leverage. What does that mean in practical terms for your current relationships with lost friends? Journal your thoughts.

THE SUSTAINED-INFLUENCE PRINCIPLE

Day TWO

🗩 Text

Read Luke 19:1–10.

🗩 Test

Why was Zacchaeus a "relational risk" to Jesus? How did Jesus approach this risk? _____

_____

_____

_____

_____

How did Zacchaeus respond to Jesus? _____

_____

_____

_____

🗩 Point

Three laws of acceptance govern the degree of influence you have with your friends:

1. The Law of Sacrifice

Many years ago Shane Claiborne of the Philadelphia-based ministry The Simple Way arrived in Calcutta, India, to apprentice under Mother Teresa. Noticing that the diminutive nun's feet were grotesquely deformed, he asked one of the sisters what had happened. The sister answered, "Mother Teresa's feet were not born like that. When people give shoes, she always waits to the very end and takes the shoes that no one else wants." Over time her feet had twisted and contorted to take the shape of ill-fitted footwear.[1]

Mother Teresa served those who needed God the most, even at the risk of her own comfort. And in that process, she carved an incredible path of influence. She operated under the Law of Sacrifice: We are open to the influence of those who serve by making a sacrifice for something we consider important; we are closed to the influence of those who are unwilling to sacrifice when sacrifice is deemed necessary.

2. The Law of Empathy

People don't behave a certain way without a reason. They don't think the way they do without a reason. There is a "why" behind your lost friends' "what"—a reason behind their actions, habits, and lifestyles. The question is, do you care enough to listen for it?

Acceptance means listening—really listening—to those who need God the most.

And listening leads to the second law of acceptance: the Law of Empathy. This law states that we are open to the influence of those who demonstrate an understanding of where we are and how we feel; we are closed to the influence of those who communicate insensitivity to our situation. You may have the exact insight or knowledge your lost friend needs to live a transformed life; but unless the Law of Empathy is in operation, he or she probably won't receive it.

3. The Law of Beginnings

Acceptance also means becoming active in the lives of those who need God the most. Lauren is a strong Christian who has a close, longtime friendship with a girl who is not a believer. Whenever this friend is in trouble, Lauren is

THE SUSTAINED–INFLUENCE PRINCIPLE

the first person to respond to her call for help. Many nights Lauren has found her friend intoxicated and puking over the toilet, and she has stayed to take care of her. She has listened to her friend talk endlessly about boyfriend woes and lifestyle issues.

Lauren knows that her participation in her friend's life is building a super-highway of influence. And one day, in God's timing, the evidence of her influence will reap eternal benefits. It's the Law of Beginnings: We are open to the influence of those who are there first; we are closed to the influence of those who come along too late.

Are you serving, listening, and being active in the lives of those friends who need God the most? Be honest and journal your thoughts and feelings.

Day THREE

💬 Text

Read Colossians 3:23–24.

💬 Test

According to Paul, how should you approach everything you do—school, work, relationships? What are the benefits of living this way?

_____

_____

_____

_____

_____

_____

_____

How do you think this kind of living would influence the people around you? _____

_____

_____

_____

_____

_____

💬 Point

Another ingredient of sustained influence is competence. We are open to the influence of people we respect because of their competence in a particular arena; we are closed to the influence of those for whom we have lost respect (or never respected in the first place). We are open to the influence of those

THE SUSTAINED-INFLUENCE PRINCIPLE

whose words are supported by their actions; we are closed to the influence of those whose actions contradict their words.

Your influence with certain friends hinges on your competency. That means, as Paul implies in Colossians 3:23–24, you must work to excel in whatever arena God has planted you. Even if you think that what you're doing has no eternal value (does it really matter if you do your best on that chemistry lab or try your hardest at soccer practice?), it does have eternal implications. Your friends are more likely to be open to your influence if they perceive that you are competent at what you do.

> **Jesus asks us to channel the competence he's given us toward others.**

Besides, you honor God whenever you recognize and make full use of the strength, resources, and gifts he has given you. You honor him by asking these questions continually throughout your life: "How can I harness all that I am, all that I have, and all that I can do for the purposes of God? How can I apply my skill, reputation, network, or resources in a way that brings honor to God? How can I take my competence and leverage it for God's sake in the lives of others?"

Consider this: In our culture and in Scripture, hands are a symbol of strength, power, and competence. Jesus used his hands to feed the hungry, heal the sick, hold little children, wash dirty feet, and touch lepers and corpses. Through his hands he displayed his unparalleled competence as a leader, teacher, and savior. But at the end of Jesus' life on earth, his hands were drawn up into helpless, grotesque claws as nails were pounded into his wrists, right through the carpal tunnel that houses the finger-controlling

tendons. When he rose from the dead, the only leftovers from the trauma of crucifixion were the nail scars in his hands:

A reminder of how he spent his life.

A reminder of where he focused his energy.

A reminder that he did not come to be served but to serve and give his life.

Jesus channeled his competence, power, and strength in our direction, for our good, and he asks us to do likewise: to channel the competence, power, and strength he has given us toward others.

How will you respond to Jesus' challenge? Is it possible to harness your competence for your own sake and at the same time claim to be a follower of the one whose strength was poured out for you? Write your answer here.

_____

_____

_____

_____

_____

_____

_____

_____

_____

_____

_____

_____

_____

_____

_____

_____

THE SUSTAINED-INFLUENCE PRINCIPLE

Day
FOUR

💬 Text

Read Matthew 5:14–16.

💬 Test

What is Paul referring to when he says "in the same way"? What comparison is he making? _____

_____

_____

_____

_____

How do you gain leverage and influence by "letting your light shine"? __

_____

_____

_____

_____

_____

_____

PART TWO:
THE PRINCIPLES

💬 Point

The final component of sustained influence is authenticity, which is defined as consistency between what we say and what we do—between what we claim to be and who we really are. Jesus was so influential because he was exactly who he claimed to be. Those who knew him best were the ones who trusted him most. What a great litmus test for authenticity!

We resist the influence of people who are not what they claim to be. Inconsistency between what is said and what is done cripples influence. Very few of us are willing to follow someone who is a blatant contradiction in terms. We're not open to their influence because they're not real; we can't trust them.

In Matthew 5:16 Jesus makes this challenge: "Let your light shine before men *in such a way* that they may see your good works, and glorify your Father who is in heaven" (NASB, emphasis added).

Notice the added emphasis: "*in such a way.*" The implication is that your life should be lived with such authenticity that your friends take notice and begin to model your lifestyle. In *The Message Remix*, Eugene Peterson paraphrases verse 16 so beautifully when he says, "By opening up to others, you'll prompt people to open up with God, this generous Father in heaven."

Your lost peers are watching you, and they want to find duplicity. They figure that if they can find a contradiction between what you say and what you do, then they're off the hook. If they see a lack of authenticity, your potential for influence in their lives is diminished. You earn influence, however, if they see you consistently walking your talk.

Perhaps you're wondering, "Should relationships really have an agenda? I mean, to try to achieve sustained influence in the lives of my friends just so I can share the gospel with them—doesn't that reek of insincerity? It almost seems underhanded! It makes friendship seem like little more than a ploy."

Allow us to answer that question with this question: Was Jesus being underhanded when he did all that he did in order to accomplish his agenda? Was he being insincere when he was busy loving people and convincing them he was the Messiah?

The answer depends on what his agenda was. The same is true for you. What's your agenda? If there is some kind of "gotcha" attached to it, then absolutely, it's underhanded and wrong. If you are somehow profiting off someone coming to faith in Christ, then your agenda is insincere and you

THE SUSTAINED-INFLUENCE PRINCIPLE

have moved into dangerous waters. There is no quota system. You're not collecting points to go to Disney World based on the influence you gain in your friends' lives. If your agenda of sustained influence has any fraction of selfish gain as a part of its makeup, you need to step back and rethink it.

The reason you should be leveraging your influence with your friends over time is that you have the cure for life's three biggest problems: sin, sorrow, and death. God has entrusted you, as his follower and ambassador, with that cure. How can you keep that cure to yourself? Sharing it with the people around you must be the driving motivation of your heart and life.

What is that cure? Jesus.

Is sharing Jesus the driving motivation in your relationships with your lost friends? If not, what is? Journal your thoughts.

Day FIVE

🗨 Text

Read John 8:1–11.

🗨 Test

How do you think this woman caught in adultery expected Jesus to respond to her when she was first brought to him? _____

_____

_____

_____

_____

_____

How was his response different from what she expected? How do you think this affected her?_____

_____

_____

_____

_____

_____

🗨 Point

One of your primary goals as a student of influence is to produce dissonance in your lost friends. *Dissonance* is the technical term for the cognitive, emotional, physiological, and behavioral state that develops when things don't go the way you expect them to. A better term might be *emotional static*. When you experience emotional static, you get a sense of mild confusion, a feeling of interruption: "What? What was that? I don't get it. Wait a minute!" You feel upset, anxious, a bit out of control. On a physiological level, your heart rate elevates, your blood pressure goes up, and your hands get sweaty. It's not a pleasant state. If Merck or Pfizer made a pill that gave people dissonance, no one would buy it. The only thing anyone ever wants to do with dissonance is get rid of it.

Right now your lost friends have a relatively comfortable set of expectations about the world and how it works. Their lives have a certain measure of consistency that they've grown accustomed to. Dissonance is manageable, and they'd like to keep it that way. The last thing they want to do is change their thinking and mess with their comfort level.

> **You need to be the consistency in the midst of unbelievers' inconsistencies.**

But change is exactly what has to happen if they are ever going to come to faith in Christ. And that's where you come in. Your job is to live your life and interact in such a way that you create a sense of inconsistency—a feeling that something doesn't quite measure up—in your lost friends.

Inconsistencies are a necessary factor in the process of influence. Conversely, they are also a big reason why teenagers hesitate to give their lives to Christ. For your lost friends to trust in Jesus, they will have to face many inconsistencies in their lives. Those inconsistencies will produce dissonance. If the inconsistencies are significant, and if you're not there close by to help them wade through them, the static could become so overwhelming that it could drown out all thoughts of belief.

That's why it's so imperative for you to develop sustained influence in your friends' lives. You can't be a flash in the pan. Most lost students will have to trek across a desert of inconsistencies to arrive at the oasis of belief. And they will need you beside them to even begin to attempt such a journey. They

will need you to love and accept them unconditionally, regardless of the inconsistencies or differences that arise. They will need you to be the consistency in the midst of their inconsistencies.

Unfortunately, most Christian students don't create enough emotional or spiritual static to gain the leverage of sustained influence. They're unable to generate dissonance because their lives are too consistent with the lives of their lost friends. How consistent is your life with the lives of the unbelievers around you? Are you creating dissonance? Journal your response.

_____

_____

_____

_____

_____

_____

_____

_____

_____

_____

_____

_____

_____

_____

_____

_____

_____

_____

THE SUSTAINED-INFLUENCE PRINCIPLE

EXP One of Mother Teresa's first projects in Calcutta, India, was to turn a former hostel into a hospice where the poor, who often died alone in the streets, could spend their last hours in comfort and cleanliness. From the start, the Catholic sisters faced alienation and neighborhood hostility, much of it emanating from the Hindu temple next door. The poor and dying have bad karma, according to Hindu belief, and the Hindu priests felt that caring for such people only interrupted their destined and ordained end.

The priests tried to get city authorities to relocate the newly named Nirmal Hriday, or "Home for the Dying." But then one of the priests was found to be in the advanced stages of tuberculosis. Denied a bed in a city hospital—beds were limited in number and reserved for those who could be cured—this representative of the enemies of the Catholic order ended up in a corner of Nirmal Hriday, tended by Mother Teresa herself. When the priest died, she delivered his body to the temple for Hindu rites. News of this charity filtered out into the city, and Calcutta started its long love affair with Mother Teresa and the humble sisters.[2]

PART TWO:
THE PRINCIPLES

Mother Teresa's story is a perfect illustration of what consistency over time can achieve. Her unconditional acceptance of even her enemies—people who wanted to destroy her—gained her great leverage in Calcutta and eventually around the world. Her competence in hospice care was unrivaled. She was everything and more than she claimed she was. She became a living, tangible example of the heart of God to millions upon millions of people. Now, Mother Teresa didn't have the opportunity to share Christ personally with every one of those millions of people. And certainly, many of the people she touched never accepted Christ as Savior and Lord. But her influence and leverage was unmistakable.

Even if the teenagers around you choose not to believe your message about God's gift of salvation through Jesus, may it be said of you that you have been the most accepting, competent, and authentic student any of them have ever known. Such qualities may not get you immediate results; but rest assured they will lead you into the kind of sustained influence that will eventually change your world.

This weekend go to God in prayer and ask him to search your heart. How accepting are you? How competent? How authentic? Pray that the Holy Spirit will increase your leverage among your lost friends by strengthening you in each of these areas.

THE SUSTAINED–INFLUENCE PRINCIPLE

Principle

You must properly put into practice the leverage you gain.

Critical Question

Are you using wisdom to leverage your
influence for the sake of the gospel?

Key Passage

1 Corinthians 15:12–20

PRINCIPLE 6

The Leverage Principle
Using Your Influence Wisely

The spiritual man habitually makes eternity judgments
instead of time judgments. Such a man would rather
be useful than famous and would
rather serve than be served.

A. W. Tozer

The Leverage Principle
Using Your Influence Wisely

Why do so few teenagers come to Christ these days? The problem isn't the gospel message. The problem is that most Christian students have zero leverage with their peers. The gospel hasn't lost its power; Christian students have lost the ability to influence their lost friends. They are failing to build relational bridges strong enough to bear the weight of truth.

As a student who desires to be influential, you need to understand this: Without a real, viable relational bridge in place, your efforts to relay truth to your unbelieving friends will be difficult at best. At worst your friends will be so turned off that they will never listen to a Christian again. But when you focus on building a relational bridge, your job gets a whole lot easier. We can almost guarantee that as you gain influence this way, opportunities will open up for you to talk about your faith, ask hard questions, and challenge your lost friends' belief systems.

Of course, leverage gained and never used is no leverage at all. You must come to a point of *trusting the trust* you have established with your unbelieving friends. Then you must exert and extend your leverage with wisdom and care.

You can do this most effectively by understanding and recognizing the two relatively distinct modes of thinking that your friends employ. The first, the systematic mode, refers to critical thinking. The thought processes of systematic thinkers are active, creative, and alert. These are the students who find holes in your testimony and ask trick questions that cause you to doubt your own salvation!

The second mode of thinking is heuristic. Students in this mode are not thinking carefully; they're skimming along the surface of ideas. They are aware of what you are saying to them, but they are not thinking conscientiously enough to catch any flaws, errors, or inconsistencies in your statements.

This current generation of students is extremely flexible in its thinking ability. Your friends can move back and forth between the two modes, often depending upon situational and personality factors. This means that no single factor (except for the Holy Spirit) is a guaranteed path to leading an unbelieving student to trust in Christ. Depending upon an individual teenager's mode of thinking, some things will work and others won't.

When your friend is in the systematic mode, for example, certain things will be influential: facts, evidence, examples, reasoning, logic—what we call *apologetics*. When your friend is in the heuristic mode, however, apologetics will be ineffective. Facts, evidence, and reasoning require too much cognitive effort. Easier-to-process information—things like attractiveness, friendliness, or excellence—will work better. We call such things *clues*.

Since different types of spiritual leverage will have different effects on different kinds of thinkers, it's crucial for you to learn to "read" your friends, determine their mode of thinking, and tailor your influence to meet their particular needs. How do you do this? That's the question we're going to try to answer over the next five days.

Day
ONE

Text

Read 1 Timothy 1:3–7.

Test

What is Paul's concern in these verses? _____

_____

_____

_____

_____

What were certain people doing that made them negative influences on others? _____

_____

_____

_____

_____

_____

_____

PART TWO:
THE PRINCIPLES

Point

When your friends are thinking systematically, they need apologetics to process the claims of Christianity in their own minds. But which set of facts, arguments, and evidence will be most effective in reaching them? That depends upon the particular questions each one has about faith in Christ. "Relative apologetics" may seem like a contradiction in terms, but it expresses this important concept.

Consider teenagers and smoking. In the past, persuasion sources (parents, teachers, the federal government) have tried to prevent teenage smoking by offering health-based evidence: "Smoking causes cancer." A statement on every pack of cigarettes gives facts and the surgeon general's opinion on the health-related perils of smoking. Yet many of your peers continue to smoke. Why? The health argument doesn't grab them. It doesn't seem relevant. They embrace the myth of their own immortality; they believe they will live forever—maybe even to forty. Threats of cancer and early death are empty to them.

> **Know the questions your friends are asking and tailor your answers for relevance.**

Newer approaches are using different arguments, however, and they are getting better results. The new arguments are based on social factors: "You will smell bad if you smoke." "No one wants to kiss somebody with cigarette breath." The importance of peer acceptance and approval makes these arguments much more relevant and powerful. It is not that the facts and evidence about the perils of smoking have changed; it's that the public service announcers have chosen to attack the problem from a more relevant angle.

Here's the point: To effectively leverage your influence, you must know the questions your friend is asking and tailor your apologetics for relevance.

One of the most difficult things about Christianity is that, on the surface, it seems like a lot of wishful thinking—a hope-filled dream that when we die, everything will work out. This is why, when you try to talk to your lost friends about your faith, you often get this response: "That's good for you, but here's what I believe . . ." The tendency is for your friends to think that Christianity is just one of many good world religions.

But Christianity is not just one more good religion. It is distinct in a number of ways. For one thing, most world religions believe you have to be good

THE LEVERAGE PRINCIPLE

and do good things to get to heaven; Christianity says you can be bad and still get to heaven (through the forgiveness of sins). You'd think that alone would make more teenagers want to come to Christ!

The most significant distinctive about Christianity, however, is one that often gets overlooked. We'll talk about it on Day Two. For today, think of one of your lost friends and write out your answers to these questions: What mode of thinking is your friend using? What are the questions he or she is asking? How can you make faith in Christ relevant to this friend?

PART TWO:
THE PRINCIPLES

Day
TWO

💬 Text

Read 1 Corinthians 15:12–20.

💬 Test

Why is the resurrection of Christ foundational to Christianity? _____

_____

_____

_____

_____

What would be the status of our faith if the resurrection did not take place?

_____

_____

_____

_____

_____

_____

💬 Point

Contrary to popular belief, the foundation of our faith is not the teachings of Jesus Christ. The teachings of Jesus are extremely important, of course; but the fact is, all world religions are based on *somebody's* teachings. No, the foundation—the primary distinction—of our faith is an event: the resurrection of Jesus Christ.

Think about it. All other world religions started with a prophet, leader, or group of people who died, either through martyrdom or natural means. Their disciples said, "Keep the dream alive!" and began spreading the teachings of their dead prophet or teacher or group.

THE LEVERAGE PRINCIPLE

You know what Jesus' followers did when Christ was crucified? They got so discouraged that they went back to fishing. They figured that with Jesus dead, it was all over. They were so afraid that they huddled in a room, scared to death. Keep the dream alive? They were thinking, *Keep* me *alive!*

Yet here we are, over two thousand years later, not because of what Jesus said, not because of the miracles he did, not even because he died on the cross. We are here because after he died, people saw a dead man walking. Jesus Christ rose from the dead and appeared to over five hundred people in the forty days after his resurrection.

> **People are afraid of death—not so much of *being* dead, but *getting* dead.**

In that time period, thousands of Jewish people in Jerusalem, the heart of Judaism, abandoned hundreds of years of heritage and embraced Christianity. Why? Because people were walking through the streets of the city saying, "I saw him!" The cowards who ran when Jesus was arrested, who denied knowing him when confronted, who refused to be present at his death, were now claiming that he was alive, and they were boldly preaching the Good News!

That's the reason Paul exclaims, "And if Christ has not been raised [from the dead], our preaching is useless and so is your faith" (1 Corinthians 15:14).

How much more leverage could you want? Jesus rose from the dead to verify his identity and validate our faith. And if a guy can rise from the dead, I don't care what he's teaching—I'm with him! He could tell me to wear a grass skirt and puka beads and run up and down the beach singing the theme from *Sponge Bob*, and I am doing it. You conquer death, and I am following you. Why? I don't want to die! I'm afraid of death—not so much of *being* dead, but *getting* dead.

PART TWO:
THE PRINCIPLES

And so are your lost friends. When they're thinking systematically, the resurrection of Jesus is the best distinctive you have to share with them.

How can you use the leverage of the resurrection with your lost friends? Journal your thoughts and thank God that the grave is empty!

THE LEVERAGE PRINCIPLE

Day THREE

💬 Text

Read Isaiah 40:12–20.

💬 Test

What picture of God do you get from these verses? _____

_____

_____

_____

What do you think Isaiah was trying to communicate about God when he penned these words? _____

_____

_____

_____

_____

_____

_____

💬 Point

**PART TWO:
THE PRINCIPLES**

What if your lost friend won't budge out of the heuristic mode? Is it still possible to find a point of leverage with a heuristic thinker? Absolutely. That's what clues are for.

Clues can be very powerful. Think about beer commercials, for example. No reasonable person would claim that attractive young women in skimpy clothes are arguments for drinking beer (unless you believe that the girls come with the six-pack). Such images certainly don't turn audiences into systematic thinkers about comparative beer quality. No, putting pretty girls in the ads simply offer a clue. People (usually guys) watch the beer commercials and see the girls. They like what they see in a way that requires little thinking on their part. And they simply associate that good feeling with beer.

Influence without thought. It works!

You can exercise leverage with your heuristic-thinking friends in a similar way. By living a magnificent life of beauty, joy, and peace, you can make Christianity too attractive for your friends to ignore. By using word pictures that describe how great God is, you can get and keep their attention.

Consider Isaiah 40:12–20, for example. What a picture! Our Creator is so huge that he can pick up the oceans of the world in the hollow of

> **By living a magnificent life, you can make Christianity too attractive to ignore.**

his hand. He can carry the dust of the earth around in a beach pail. He's so wise that no one ever has to tell him what to do. He doesn't have to attend Harvard Business School to learn how to be God.

In this passage Isaiah gives heuristic thinkers a picture of God. Then in verse 18, he confronts them with a choice: "To whom, then, will you compare God? What image will you compare him to?"

You can lead your heuristic-thinking friends to a similar moment of reckoning. Whether by words or implication, when you present God in all his glory, you ask, "Isn't our God huge, wonderful, amazing, beautiful? Who can compare—that jock who thinks he owns the football field? The guy who thinks he's God's gift to the opposite sex? The gorgeous girl who just won homecoming queen? That computer geek who's so smart, he could break into Fort Knox with his laptop?"

THE LEVERAGE PRINCIPLE

What a clue! Scripture, nature, life and all of its lessons—they are chock full of clues about God that you can point your friends to. If you aren't sure what mode of thinking a particular friend is using, remember this:

What to do? Get a clue.

It's always wise to paint a beautiful picture of God's greatness and might. It's always right to paint a beautiful picture of the compassion and wisdom of Jesus. When you lift Jesus up, he will draw people to himself. That's his promise in John 12:32. Even systematic thinkers can't help but be moved.

What clues about God or Jesus are likely to have the most powerful impact on your lost friends? Write them down here.

**PART TWO:
THE PRINCIPLES**

_____

_____

_____

_____

_____

_____

_____

_____

_____

_____

_____

_____

_____

_____

_____

_____

_____

Day FOUR

🗨 Text

Read Matthew 9:9-13

🗨 Test

What do you notice about Jesus calling Matthew to follow Him? What did He do to cause Matthew to follow Him? _____

_____

_____

How did Jesus pattern His question to the Pharisees? What is important to you about the way Jesus asked the question and what He asked?_____

_____

_____

_____

🗨 Point

There are six important principles that relate to the leverage you bring to bear with your lost friends:

1. Learn to "read" your unbelieving friends.

The student who is adept at "reading" their friends will be more likely to use leverage effectively. If you can figure out the mental state of your unbelieving friend, you've taken a giant step toward success. But how can you judge another person's mental state?

2. Learn to observe nonverbal behavior.

Generally speaking, if you observe behavior that indicates attentiveness, alertness, and thoughtfulness, you can begin to assume your friend is in the systematic mode. As you see behavior that demonstrates distraction, boredom, or laziness, you can assume that your friend is in the heuristic mode.

THE LEVERAGE PRINCIPLE

3. Learn the art of asking pertinent questions.

Get your friend to respond. Then judge the quality of the responses. Do they sound thoughtful and reasonable? Or does your friend ask you to repeat the question or give answers that are off the wall?

4. Learn to match the right influence tool with the correct mental state.

You don't need an umbrella on a sunny day, and students that think heuristically will not heed apologetics. You have to identify correctly what your friend's mental state is, then provide either apologetics or clues.

This is probably the biggest mistake we make in our attempts to use the spiritual leverage we have obtained. It can be extremely frustrating to develop great arguments or clues, but then see them fail because you used them at the wrong time. Using leverage wisely means that you are adept at connecting the right influence tool to the mental state of your unbelieving friend.

5. When in doubt, take the peripheral route.

More times than not, your friends will be in the heuristic mode. You have probably been conditioned to exert leverage in a systematic mode. We often make the unfortunate error of assuming that an unbelieving friend is thinking the same way we are. So what do we do? We go off with all the great arguments about why somebody should change. And how does our friend respond: "That's cool. Could you pass the salsa, dude?" They weren't willing and able to think systematically, and all our hard work is down the tubes.

A major part of disciplism is the process of moving a friend from heuristic to systematic thinking. This is not to say that you should not use evidence and facts. But first we must make sure that our friends are willing and able to do the needed thinking. If you cannot assure yourself that an unbelieving friend is in such a frame of mind, it is useless and frustrating to try and influence with evidence and facts.

6. Develop arguments from the point of view of your lost friends.

The worst arguments are usually the ones we prefer. We tend to offer arguments that are compelling and powerful to us. Accordingly, we tend to assume that other people will respond the same way we do. That's a bad assumption.

The best way for you to develop leverage is to carefully observe your friends. Really listen to them. Ask them about the music they like and the movies they watch. Pay attention to the clothes they wear and the language they use. People who tune into others will develop an intuitive sense of what makes for effective evidence and what makes for an ineffective argument.

Of these six principles, which do you think Jesus capitalized on most? Which of these do you think you need to use more effectively? Journal your thoughts.

THE LEVERAGE PRINCIPLE

Day FIVE

💬 Text

Read Romans 10:14–15.

💬 Test

What is the process that Paul lays out for someone to become a Christian?

_____

_____

_____

What is your role in this process? _____

_____

_____

_____

_____

_____

💬 Point

Disciplism involves building a bridge of relationship with your lost friends and then using the appropriate leverage to move them across that bridge one step at a time. The type of leverage that you use depends upon where your friends are in this five-step process:

Step One: "Huh?"

At this step students have never heard of Jesus. Never seen a Bible. They have no clue what this gospel thing is all about. Also at this step are all those teenagers who know something about Jesus but see absolutely no reason to respond to him. Most of your unbelieving friends are probably at this step.

Step Two: "Oh!"

At this step students have heard the gospel. They've seen the difference Jesus can make in a person's life, and they realize there may be something to Christianity. They want to borrow your Bible or go to youth group with you. They begin to talk to you about God stuff.

Step Three: "What?"

Teenagers at this step are weighing their options. They are carefully evaluating what they will lose and gain by trusting in Christ. Don't rush them or use "Stupid Church Tricks" at this point to try to persuade them to trust Christ. Rather, be patient, hang in there, and exert leverage only according to the pace at which they are crossing the bridge.

Step Four: "OK!"

Students take this step when they are willing and ready to trust Christ with their lives. This is the moment you have worked so hard for. It deserves to be celebrated! Heaven throws a party. So should you!

But don't give your friends the idea that they've crossed the finish line. Trusting in Christ as Lord and Savior definitely determines their eternal destination. But it doesn't guarantee them the eternal life that the New Testament talks about—the eternal life that refers to their quality of life in Christ on earth. They still have one more step.

Step Five: "Let's Go!"

Step Five is the process of transformation in which the Christ-life becomes more and more the normal way for your friends to live. How long does it take? That depends. Many of your friends have come to Christ with serious

THE LEVERAGE PRINCIPLE

baggage. Others have horrible, hard-to-break habits. Still others have been deeply involved in extreme lifestyles. If renewal were as simple as learning to use a DVD player, they would get it down almost instantaneously. But real transformation is much more significant. It takes time.

How many weeks, months, or years will it take your friends to get from Step One to Step Five? We don't know. But we do know this: Whatever the length of the journey, you must travel it with them, and you must do it one step at a time.

Think of one lost friend in your life. Where is he or she in this five-step process? How can you move your friend to the next step? Journal your thoughts.

_____

_____

_____

_____

_____

_____

_____

PART TWO:
THE PRINCIPLES

_____

_____

_____

_____

_____

_____

_____

_____

EXP Kelsey's freshman year of college promised to be a major adjustment, to say the least. She had decided to go to school away from home, which meant living on a campus and in a town where she didn't know a soul.

The school assigned her a roommate: a Hindu girl named Pratima. Pratima's family was originally from India but moved to the United States so their daughter could receive a better education. The girls' first night together was full of conversation. Kelsey was intrigued but a bit uneasy with the chants Pratima had written on the bathroom mirror, the Hindu figurines she had placed around the room, and the potent smell of curry that permeated the air. They discussed religion and, to Kelsey's surprise, Pratima knew as much about Jesus as Kelsey did. In fact, Pratima was very knowledgeable about Christianity—she just wasn't interested in following it. She was devoutly Hindu.

Over the next few weeks, Kelsey made several unsuccessful attempts to persuade Pratima to accept her way of thinking. Kelsey had witnessed to people before; she had even led people to Christ before. But she couldn't budge Pratima. *Why is she so challenging?* Kelsey wondered.

One reason: They were roommates, and Pratima was watching Kelsey day in and day out. Each evening when Kelsey had her quiet time, for example, Pratima took note. One night Kelsey came in very late and decided that at that moment, sleep was more appealing than spending time with God. As she slithered into her bed, Pratima (who Kelsey had assumed was sound asleep) spoke up from her bed on the other side of the room. "You didn't spend time with your God today," she said matter-of-factly, her face turned to the wall.

Kelsey immediately jerked up in bed and turned on her bedside lamp. "You're right, I didn't. Thank you," she said, opening her Bible.

At that moment Kelsey realized something important: The point of her

THE LEVERAGE PRINCIPLE

relationship with Pratima was not to persuade her with clever arguments to choose Christianity. It was to live the Christ-life in front of her in a way that would cause her to crave it.

Kelsey had never been faced with such a monumental challenge: to live a life of godly standards, right priorities, accountability, and unconditional acceptance before another person over a sustained period of time. To be in the midst of maximum dynamic pressure and not only survive but thrive.

She spent an entire semester gaining leverage with Pratima and then learning how to exert that leverage effectively. She learned how to ask pertinent questions that forced Pratima to defend and question her own belief system. Sometimes simply pointing to the beauty of God was influence enough. At other times she and Pratima engaged in serious dialogue about the evidence and proof of Christ's resurrection.

Much time passed before Pratima began going to a worship gathering of college students that Kelsey attended. Eventually Pratima started attending a Bible study with Kelsey, where she asked many hard-hitting questions. By the time their living arrangement ended, Pratima was open to the idea of accepting Christ.

We guarantee that at some point you will have a Pratima in your life. This person may not be a person of a different religion or culture, but might be a classmate, a neighbor, or a teammate who needs to know Jesus. This weekend consider this question: Are you ready and willing to leverage your life for the name and fame of God?

**PART TWO:
THE PRINCIPLES**

The key to successful leadership today
is influence, not authority.

KENNETH BLANCHARD

Epilogue

The joke is told that at the beginning of the 2003 military conflict in Iraq, Secretary of State Colin Powell put a haughty Iraqi reporter in his place.

"Isn't it true that only 13 percent of young Americans can locate Iraq on a map?" the reporter asked.

"That may be true," Secretary Powell answered. "You're probably right. But unfortunately for you, all 13 percent are marines."

God is not concerned with the *quantity* of students who desire to be influential. His concern is with the *quality* of students. He is not looking for influential students he can make faithful. He is looking for faithful students he can make influential.

When the young Americans who know their geography are marines, *how many* is irrelevant. And when the teenagers who take on the hurricane force of maximum dynamic pressure are Christian students of godly standards, right priorities, maintained accountability, unconditional acceptance, and sustained influence, *how many* is irrelevant.

The lives of countless numbers of your peers—teenagers who are hurting, petrified, and confused—are breaking apart daily under the pressure of Max Q.

Someone has to have the love and the courage to rescue them. Will it be you?

Notes

Introduction

Epigraph. Jim Rayburn III, *Dance, Children, Dance* (Wheaton, Ill.: Tyndale House Publishers, 1984), 158.

Week 1: Granting Permission

Epigraph. John Eldredge, *Wild at Heart* (Nashville: Thomas Nelson Publishing, 2001), 149.

1. From an interview with Josh McDowell at the May 2003 GrowUp Conference at North Point Community Church. The session was titled "Be Relevant."

2. *First Knight*, Columbia Pictures, 1995. Written by Lorne Cameron, David Hoselton, and William Nicholson. Directed by Jerry Zucker.

Week 2: Knowing What to Expect

Epigraph. Erwin Raphael McManus, *An Unstoppable Force* (Loveland, Colo.: Group Publishing, 2001).

1. From copyrighted resource material by Reggie Joiner, "Be Relevant," http://www. 252Basics.org, http://www.GrowUponline.com, (2003).

Week 3: Understanding Influence

1. Jeff Cannon and Lt. Cdr. Jon Cannon, *Leadership Lessons of the Navy Seals* (New York: McGraw-Hill, 2003), 31.

Part Two: The Principles

1. This is one of those urban legends that has circulated for years in various forms across the Internet. Some versions say the American scientists were from the Federal Aviation Administration; other versions say they were from the Air Force. In some versions the British engineers are not British at all but from France or even America. Whatever the truth is, the point is still the same!

Week 6: The Priorities Principle

Epigraph. John Eldredge, *Waking the Dead* (Nashville: Thomas Nelson Publishing, 2003), 211.

Week 7: The Accountabilty Principle

1. Gregory Lumberg, "When Love Comes to Town," *CCM*, January 2001.
2. Mike Krzyzewski, *Leading from the Heart* (New York: Warner Books, 2000), 11.

Week 8: The Unconditional-Acceptance Principle

Epigraph. G. K. Chesterton, *Orthodoxy* (San Francisco: Ignatius Press, 1908), 55.

Week 9: The Sustained-Influence Principle

Epigraph. Janet Chismar, "Louie Giglio: Shaping a New Generation through OneDay03," http://www.crosswalk.com/fun/music/1198424.html.
1. Trinity Church Web site, "Don't Lose Your Footing," http://www.trinitytoledo.org/pdf/upload/SermoneEaster3B.pdf.
2. Subir Bhaumik and Meenakshi Ganguly, "Seeker of Souls," *Time*, September 15, 1997.

NOTES